is revolution change?

edited by brian griffiths

inter-varsity press
downers grove, illinois 60515

© 1972 by
Inter-Varsity Press,
London. First
American printing,
February 1972,
by InterVarsity Press
with permission
from Inter-Varsity
Fellowship, England

InterVarsity Press
is the book publishing
division of
Inter-Varsity Christian
Fellowship.

ISBN 0-87784-545-X
Library of Congress
Catalog Card
Number: 74-186350

Printed in the
United States of
America

Contents

Preface

Despite the increasing affluence and remarkable technological achievements of recent years, we live in a world of intense dissatisfaction – dissatisfaction with gadgets, with food in tin cans, with convention, with imperialism and neo-imperialism, with war games and real battles, with bureaucracy and with traditional religion. Even on the fringes of our society one cannot escape the urban bourgeois 'happening'. The need is for something radical, something totally different – violent revolution, an unstructured hippie community, the exploration of the occult.

These essays have been put together in the belief that none of these alternatives is radical enough; that the only really radical solution is a faith centred in Jesus Christ, a faith which is not simply for the cloistered, pietistic cell, but which affects all areas of life, not least our responsibility in society at large.

The five chapters in this symposium were written entirely independently of each other, without any thought of putting them together in such a volume as this. But they were written because each of the authors felt compelled to speak out against the fantasy of revolution. If the book has a unifying theme, it is that a violent and total revolution is no panacea for society's problems. The crucial weakness underlying the non-Christian alternatives is their unrealistic assessment of human nature, man himself. But this should not make the Christian complacent and smug, a supporter of the *status quo*. As this book will show, he has a clear mandate to be involved in the society of which he is part, to help the under-privileged and to challenge injustice whenever he finds it.

Because these essays were written independently of each other not surprisingly they overlap to some extent. On some issues they disagree. And this is how it should be. For while each is in complete agreement in affirming the relevance of the Christian faith, that same faith does not provide a unique political programme to right the world. It makes sweeping statements about the nature of man and society, mandates its followers to do all things in the spirit of Christian love, but never provides a specific programme of action to deal with the Vietnam war, the extent of immigration, the process of de-colonization or any other particular political issue.

In an era which boasts intellectual integrity and open-mindedness, at the very least the Christian message for society deserves serious examination. Hopefully this book will make the message that much clearer and in turn its acceptance that much easier.

Brian Griffiths

1 The Law and Order Issue
Brian Griffiths

The nature of the revolt

For the university as an institution, the last decade has been
an enigma. The university has been the centre of an attack
not only on the purpose and content of higher education,
but also on the underlying values of our present Western
civilization. Ostensibly, the issues have been the war in
Vietnam, apartheid in South Africa, civil rights in the US,
fascism in Greece and the subtle techniques of repression in
most misnamed 'democracies'. But in fact these issues have
been used to initiate a much larger debate on the role of
law, the relevance of the family as a unit, the need for
authority, the potential of society and the quality of life
in our modern affluence.

The debate has not been carried on within the traditionally accepted rules of the institution. Increasingly throughout the decade, demonstrations, sit-ins and violence have
taken place in colleges and universities throughout the
world – North and South America, Japan, Pakistan and
most countries of Western Europe. Their object has been
to by-pass the tortuous procedures of bureaucracy and
democracy and instigate direct confrontation between those
with power and those with grievances. This resort to direct
action has been paralleled outside the university by the
so-called process of taking democracy into the streets. The
result has been riots in the black ghettoes of American
cities, near civil war in Ulster, the May 1968 crisis in

France, the May 1970 crisis in the United States, and clashes between demonstrators and police in most Western countries. The current situation was never better summed up than in the Black Panther slogan: '1968 – The Year of the Pig, The Death of the Ballot, The Birth of the Bullet'.

This crisis has been taken seriously in one country after another. In the UK, a Select Committee of the House of Commons was set up in 1968 to study student relations, producing a report with five accompanying volumes of evidence. In the US, President Johnson set up a Task Force on the Causes and Prevention of Violence and President Nixon has set up a special investigation into campus unrest. Similarly within most universities, the administration as well as faculties have been forced to revise their teaching programmes, student facilities and disciplinary procedures.

But this apparent disregard for authority and the increasing use of violence also produced its own reaction. In the middle of the May 1968 crisis in France, the government issued a communiqué stating that

> 'Now that university reform can be anything but a pretext to plunge the country into disorder the government has a duty to maintain public order and to protect all citizens without exception against excess and perversion',

and that

> 'the government cannot permit public order to be disrupted by actions against the national heritage and against the legitimate interests of all sections of the population'.

In an editorial in *The Times* of 5 October 1968 on 'The British Backlash', it was predicted that

> 'In Britain and perhaps in the whole world the revolt of students is producing a contrary resentment which could prove more formidable than anything the students can do. ... The danger of anarchy is likely, even in this country, to lead to a more authoritarian social life.'

In the prelude to the British General Election of 1970, as in the US 1968 Presidential Election, the need for 'law and order' was made a specific election issue.

A leading American psychologist, Bettelheim, in analysing the youth generation in America today, is more pessimistic of the backlash than of what produced it.

> 'If I read the signs of our own times correctly, I do not think that our student rebels, in and by themselves, are a serious political danger – though I deem them a real threat to the universities and to the intellectual life of our society. What I fear is rather the opposite: that the provocative behaviour of a very small group of students will arouse a dangerous counter-reaction. Their Fascism of the Left may bring on a Right backlash which could indeed strangle the democratic order.'[1]

Equally pessimistic is the philosopher, Professor Sidney Hook.

> 'The sober fact is that violence has reached such proportions on the campuses today that the whole atmosphere of American – and not a few European (not to mention Japanese) universities has been transformed. The appeal to reason is no longer sufficient to resolve problems or even to keep the peace. In order to make itself heard in some of our most prestigious institutions, the appeal to reason must finally appeal to the courts and to the police. . . . Violence in the academy is an outgrowth of violence in the streets and cities of the country. That is where the gravest danger lies.'[2]

This growth of student radicalism and violence raises much greater questions than simply the adequacy of library facilities, the price of refectory food or the cost of student housing. Underlying the present revolt against authority is a firmly held set of beliefs, whose premises are the very antithesis of the Christian understanding of man and society which has been such an important factor in the growth of Western democracies.

The purpose of this chapter is to put these ideologies and the resulting debate on 'law and order' within a Christian perspective. The present tendency, not least among certain sections of the Christian church, is to emphasize social justice to the exclusion of authority, discipline and law.

[1] Bruno Bettelheim, 'Obsolete Youth', *Encounter*, September 1969, p. 30.
[2] Sidney Hook, 'The Ideology of Violence', *Encounter*, April 1970, p. 38.

But because of the biblical emphasis on obedience to the civil authorities, the temptation for the more conservative Christian is a smug complacency even in the face of police brutality, public corruption and a political judiciary. The Christian must avoid both these extremes. While he must support the police, the executive and the judiciary in their task of enforcing the law, at the same time he must not hesitate to denounce and protest at individual and social injustice. His mandate is to be a light in society – not a mirror, simply reflecting it.

The logic of dissent

A marked characteristic of the present radical movement is the absence of any unanimously accepted ideology. In fact, the very opposite is true. The radical student movement includes a variety of political groupings. Nevertheless, apart from the sectarian differences which distinguish particular socialist groups from each other, and the existence of those who accept the basic values of a social democracy but who on specific issues would be prepared to demonstrate against property and possibly persons, there are broadly speaking three discernible systems of thought among modern dissenters – socialism, anarchism, and the hippie philosophy of love.

Socialist dissent

The basic postulate of socialism is that capitalist society can be divided into mutually exclusive interest groups or classes, based on the ownership of capital. Capital divides society into those with and those without power and influence. But capital confers on its owners more than simply economic and political power. The effects of the class division are profound and far-reaching. To Gramschi, the Italian socialist intellectual, it implies 'the dominance of one social bloc over another not simply by means of force or wealth, but by a social authority whose ultimate sanction is a profound cultural supremacy'.[3]

The division in Britain today is allegedly between the relatively few wealth owners, politically represented in the leadership of the Conservative Party, having access to, if not control of, the mass media and sharing a common educational background, and the Labour Movement as a whole. Allegedly the substantial changes in society over the past century, such as the division of ownership from management in industry, income and wealth re-distribution through a progressive system of taxation as well as the wide range of benefits offered through the Welfare State, are ineffective in re-distributing either wealth or power. They have done little either to bridge the gulf which still exists between the two irreconcilable classes in our society, the haves and the have-nots, or to offer true radicals any chance of real power.

Perry Anderson, editor of the *New Left Review*, has argued that

> 'class has eaten into every realm of social and private life. There is no neutral area into which the individual can withdraw from the dichotomized society of which he is part. He is never free. His work, his art, his sexuality, his most personal freedoms have all been distorted or confiscated by the capitalist machine.'[4]

The individual, in Marxist terminology, is 'alienated'. His experience of life is not self-determined, but dictated by his class and as a class member he is manipulated by industrial magnates, advertising men, television producers and newspaper editors. The concept of choice and freedom are fictitious. The goods he buys, the news he reads, the films he sees, the justice he faces, are all ultimately determined by the class machine, as is the way he evaluates politics, other people and ultimately himself. Talk about law and order is simply to justify the *status quo*. It is 'their' law and 'their' order. It was designed by them, legislated by them and is enforced by them. How can it be impartial?

[3] Perry Anderson, 'Origins of the Present Crisis' in P. Anderson and R. Blackburn (editors), *Towards Socialism* (Fontana, London, 1965; Cornell University Press, New York, 1966), pp. 11–52.
[4] Perry Anderson, *ibid.*

For the Marxist, superficial reforms are obviously not enough. The task is 'to create a new model of civilization, with its own values, its own relations, its own creativity'.[5] As long as a capitalist society exists, there must inevitably be a continuous struggle between the two basic classes. Society demands radical change. But how can society be changed? Broadly, there are two strategies. On the one hand, there is the belief in evolutionary change through social democracy, the basic strategy of the Fabian Society and the Labour Party. This entails accepting the framework of democracy – political parties, the winning of elections and the subsequent implementation of policy by parliamentary legislation. Such change is inevitably gradual and, for this very reason, unacceptable.

> 'Student insurgents have rejected established models of political action; they refuse to pin their hopes on the remote manoeuvres of parliamentary assemblies or party conferences. . . . In exchange for this quinquennial participation people surrender control over their everyday existence. The revolutionary student movement have denounced this capitalistic bargain as the graveyard of any hope of transforming society.'[6]

The second alternative is revolution – a head-on clash between the two interest groups. Most socialists have followed the dictate of Lenin, who on the eve of the 1917 revolution wrote that 'The substitution of the proletariat State for the bourgeois State is impossible without a violent revolution'.

An important recent socialist illustration of the theme of violence which has had substantial influence is the writings of Frantz Fanon. Born in the French Antilles, educated in a French medical school and a participant in the Algerian War, his writings deal with the psychological problems of colonized (especially black) people and their struggle for independence. Although the distinction between capitalist and proletariat is replaced by that between settler and

---

[5] Perry Anderson, *ibid.*

[6] Alexander Cockburn, 'Introduction' in A. Cockburn and R. Blackburn (editors), *Student Power: Problems, Diagnosis, Action* (Penguin Books, Harmondsworth, 1969).

native, the analysis is very much in the Marxist tradition. The settler dominates the native peasants, not only through tangible politico-economic power, but more devastatingly through a cultural and psychological domination. De-colonization is the minimum demand of colonized peoples. Its potential is enormous. Its aim is 'to change the order of the world' and, with it, it 'brings a natural rhythm into existence, introduced by new men and with it a new language and a new humanity. Decolonization is the verit-able creation of new men. But this creation owes nothing of its legitimacy to any supernatural power.'[7] By contrast with traditional Marxist analysis, it is the poor peasantry and not the urban working class which is the authentic revolution-ary force in the Third World to instigate this process.

In *The Wretched of the Earth*, the book which has achieved the most publicity, Fanon sets out in particular to ration-alize the use of violence. In the first place, violence is necessary because de-colonization is inevitably a violent phenomenon. The initial encounter between the native and the settler was a process of exploitation and pillage based on the latter's superior force, and the subsequent legitimacy of the colonial régime has been the continual appeal to force. Only violence can overcome violence, so that the counter-violence of the natives will be in direct proportion to the violence of the colonial régime.

Secondly, violence is a method of integrating and unify-ing the colonized people:

'The practice of violence binds them together as a whole, since the individual forms a violent link in the great chain, a part of the great organism of violence which has surged upwards in reaction to the settlers' violence in the begin-ning.'[8]

This is in direct contrast to colonialism which is separatist and regionalist, encouraging chieftaincies and status and re-inforcing tribalism. But in the process of de-colonization

[7] Frantz Fanon, 'Concerning Violence', *The Wretched of the Earth* (MacGibbon and Kee, London, and Grove Press, New York, 1965), pp. 27–74.
[8] This and the following quotations from Fanon's book are taken from the chapter 'Concerning Violence', pp. 27–74.

each man is introduced to the idea of a common cause, a national destiny and is aware of a collective history.

> 'Through each's participation in violence the people realize that it has been the business of each of them and that the leader has no special merit.'

The example given is that of the Mau-Mau in Kenya where it was the practice that each member of the group struck a blow at the victim, so that each one was thus personally responsible for his death. This means that outlawed members of the group can find their place once more and become integrated. 'Violence is thus seen to be comparable to a royal pardon.'

Thirdly, at the individual level, violence is a cathartic force. It liberates the colonized from his inferiority complex, despair and inactivity and restores his self-respect, making him aggressive and fearless. For the natives,

> 'Violence alone, violence committed by the people, violence organized and educated by its leaders makes it possible for the masses to understand social truths and gives the key to them.'

Violence 'invests their characters with positive and creative qualities'. This cleansing effect of force comes out in a quotation which Fanon uses from *Les Armes Miraculeuses* by Armé Cesaire, in which 'The Rebel' describes his murder of a typical colonial settler to 'The Mother':

> 'It was an evening in November . . .
> And suddenly shouts lit up the silence;
>   We had attacked, we the slaves; we, the dung underfoot, we the animals with patient hooves,
>   We were running like madmen; shots rang out . . . We were striking. Blood and sweat cooled and refreshed us. We were striking where the shouts came from, and the shouts became more strident and a great clamour rose from the east: it was the outhouses burning and the flames flickered sweetly on our cheeks.
>   Then was the assault made on the master's house.
>   They were firing from the windows.
>   We broke the doors.
>   The master's room was wide open. The master's room was brilliantly lighted, and the master was there, very

calm . . . and our people stopped dead . . . it was the master
. . . I went in. "It's you", he said, very calm.

It was I, even I, and I told him so, the good slave, the
faithful slave, the slave of slaves, and suddenly his eyes
were like two cockroaches, frightened in the rainy season . . .
I struck, and the blood spurted; that is the only baptism
that I remember today.'

This existential therapy of violence is also apparent in
Sartre's introduction to the book:

'. . . the irrepressible violence is neither sound and fury, nor
the resurrection of savage instincts, nor even the effect of
resentment; it is man re-creating himself . . . To shoot a
European is to kill two birds with one stone, to destroy an
oppressor and the man he oppresses at the same time, there
remain a dead man and a free man.'[9]

Anarchist dissent

Socialism, then, can cover a whole range of viewpoints
about the way it is to achieve its aims, including the way
of violence. Anarchism is another tradition of thought
which underlies contemporary dissent. Avowedly utopian,
its intention is to abolish not only government but any
kind of authority.

'The essence of anarchism, the one thing without which it is
not anarchism, is the negation of authority over anyone
by anyone.'[1]

For those who believe that man is essentially good, it is
easy enough to see how their only possible response to the
modern world is anarchism. It is not protesting youth but
established governments which have produced the cold
war, the stockpiling of nuclear weapons, the vast military-
industrial complexes, the excessive urbanization and the
ecological chaos for which most developed countries seem
destined. Authority is not only immoral in its use of force, it
is also incompetent.

By contrast with the imperfect present, the ideal is a

[9] Jean-Paul Sartre, 'Preface', *The Wretched of the Earth*, pp. 7–26.
[1] Nicolas Walter, *Anarchy 100*, Vol. 9, No. 6 (June 1969) (Freedom
Press), p. 164.

society with total freedom and total equality. Freedom without equality which is the result of liberalism suffers from the inequalities not only of wealth and opportunity, but also the inequality of freedom itself. The rich can buy freedom more easily than the poor. Equality without freedom on the other hand is the unfortunate history of socialism. The anarchist claim is to have perceived that, if there is no government, freedom and equality are the same thing.

Hippie dissent

By comparison with both socialism and anarchism, the hippie philosophy and the Underground sub-culture are both incoherent and nebulous. Their starting-point is the same – an intense dissatisfaction with the quality of life in our affluent societies. Modern society is repressive, full of 'plastic' people, leading empty lives, conforming to materialistic norms and afraid to deviate. The authorities, whether in the guise of police, parents or politicians, are against the young. They laugh at their clothes, deride their long hair, urge them to find employment to produce yet more useless technological gadgets, fail to understand their music, their sex patterns or the expansive influence of drugs.

The hippie approach differs from the others in that it is decidedly anti-intellectual and a-rational. Any attempt to come to grips with the outside world is doomed to failure. The outside world – Vietnam, nuclear weapons, the draft, racial exploitation – is too irrational to explain. A political programme in such a society is bound to fail, at least for the next few years. The only route left is escape. Forget about the outside world. As the Sopwith Camel put it in a song:

> 'Stamp out reality
> Before reality stamps out you.'

Life must be lived to the full, here and now. Drugs become simply a vehicle for this escape. Everyone must do his own thing. To change society is impossible. But by opting out and forming a new community such as in Haight-Asbury or Alice's Restaurant, the outside world can be shown how it ought to live. Within the community the hippie child will be reared with

> 'no birth certificate, no schooling unless the child wants it, no taxation, no official record of his existence. These children will be tranquillized by hash, lullabied by rock and roll, educated by the community.'[2]

Neville, in elaborating the ideals of such a community, lists them as: (a) drugs (pot and LSD); (b) pop music; (c) guilt-free sex; and (d) 'the politics of play'. The purpose of such a community is to provide 'an alternative way of life' and evolve 'a culture that is destined to create a new kind of man'.[3]

The tendency of most observers and especially social scientists is to stress the substantial differences between the ideologies of socialism, anarchism and the hippies. Certainly there are many differences between the three, yet from a Christian viewpoint they have a remarkable similarity. All start from the *basic premise* that human beings are essentially rational and loving; their basic nature is fundamentally good. Their potential remains unrealized not because of any defects in their make-up but because of artificial and societally imposed constraints – be they class (socialism), the existence of the State (anarchism) or urban, industrialized society (hippie). Each philosophy has a more or less (usually less) defined *Utopia*: the classless society which has rid itself of alienation, the society without the constricting apparatus of the State and the society which permits total freedom, complete individualism and love without limit. Perhaps of more importance, each also has what George Sorel, the early twentieth-century French socialist apologist of violence, called the *Myth*. This is not an analysable set of propositions describing the properties of the perfect society. Rather it is a partially defined fantasy, not susceptible to rational analysis but so powerful

---

[2] Richard Neville, *Play Power* (Jonathan Cape, London, and Paladin Press, New York, 1970), p. 56.
[3] Richard Neville, *ibid.*

that it stirs our emotions, forcing us to act. It appeals not to our reason, but to our emotions, our dreams.

Not only do these philosophies have a clearly spelt-out analysis of our modern dilemma, an Ideal by which it should be replaced, a Myth which keeps its followers following. They also have a *magic wand solution* to move from reality to the Ideal – the proletariat revolution, the violence of de-colonization, the abolition of the State or simply the hippie escape back to nature. And yet year after year passes and the Utopia is not realized; bourgeois democracies are not overthrown by revolution; there is little hope that the State will be abolished; de-colonization is the cause of wars and frequently military dictatorships prove to be the only viable form of government; the road back to nature may end in the horror of a Californian valley. There seems little that can be done except to protest against the present. The protest may be violent or non-violent. But whether it is the defendant's behaviour at a trial, a civil rights demonstration, the burning of a bank or the use of a gelignite bomb to blow up a police station in Ulster, it is an assault on existing authority, a challenge to law and order and hopefully a catalyst for change.

Is authority inevitable?

Dissenters of the present generation, as we have seen, do not accept the necessity of authority in society. Because of their faith in the reasonableness of human nature, they feel that insistence on 'law and order' is simply repressive. For a Christian, however, the answer to the question 'Is authority inevitable?' must be an unequivocal 'Yes'. A society without an authority structure is inconceivable. Unlike the non-Christian, the starting-point for the Christian is a belief neither in the innate goodness of man nor in the inevitability of progress, but in the ultimate authority of God.

The Bible's revelation of God shows Him as being totally separate and 'other' than man. His existence, knowledge, morality and power are entirely independent of

His creation. But for man the very opposite is the case. He is God's creation, not just the chance product of his environment. His faculties and personality are a reflection of those of God Himself. Because he has been created in the image of God, he has a conscience, a sense of right and wrong and a capacity for moral judgment. The fact of creation implies not only the complete dependence of man on God, but also the complete authority of God over man. The greatness of Eden was that man recognized God's authority with the result that he was at one with his environment, his society and himself. On the basis of His authority over man, God has enunciated principles by which he is to live (the Ten Commandments and the Sermon on the Mount), a way of reconciliation to Himself and ultimately a day of judgment.

But the society in which we find ourselves today is a far remove from Eden. Man's relationship to God has been distorted. In past history man decided to assert his independence and reject the total authority of God over his life. In biblical language, man fell. As a result of the Fall, every facet of man's personality – his will, his mind, his emotions, his conscience – has been distorted. In each individual, there is a continual tension between his desire to do good and his inability to fulfil that desire. His will is directed to evil as well as to good. His mind has become restricted so that he sees his dilemma solely in human terms. His emotions reach beyond his control. His conscience may become so depraved that it is unable to distinguish good from evil. For this reason, and this alone, modern society, although apparently irrational, is not inexplicable to the Christian. Neither is Auschwitz, race hatred or the atrocities of Vietnam. In the final analysis, all injustice, unrest, war and violence is the result of sin. And sin for the Christian is not the self-interest, pettiness or unconscious 'mistakes' of the collective, be it the bourgeoisie, the State or the vast majority of society, but the sinful nature of each individual and his consequently deliberately sinful actions.

From the nature of God's creation as well as the effects of the Fall, both of which are reflected in the principles enunciated in the Mosaic Law, the need for authority becomes evident in the institutions which are specifically dealt with by biblical writers, such as the family and the State.

Starting from this set of assumptions it is not surprising that writers as far removed as the prophet Daniel and the apostle Paul argue that the whole apparatus of the judiciary and the State derive their ultimate authority, whether they care to recognize it or not, from God and for that very reason demand allegiance. Paul argues that 'there is no authority but by act of God, and the existing authorities are instituted by him'.[4] This is so whether the government is elected by the people or whether it claims 'the divine right of kings'. From there he goes on to argue that anyone who rebels against authority is 'resisting a divine institution'. He specifically mentions that through the process of maintaining law and order 'the authorities are in God's service'. The appeal for Christians to support the authorities is not the obvious penalty for disobedience but for 'conscience sake', because they are the instruments of God. The prophet Daniel in interpreting Nebuchadnezzar's dream stated quite openly to him that he was 'king of kings, to whom the God of heaven has given the kingdom with all its power, authority, and honour'.[5] Of God, Daniel says that 'he deposes kings and sets them up'.[6]

The teaching of Jesus Himself on this issue is of course of crucial importance, and is also of particular relevance when it is seen against the political milieu in which Jesus found Himself. He was born in a country, Palestine, which was a colony of the vast Roman Empire. The background of His teaching and life had all the characteristics of a colonial administration – the colonial governor (Pontius Pilate), the occupying Roman army, the henchmen of Roman administration (the tax collectors) and the extreme nationalists, fighting a subversive guerilla war (the Zealots). The political choice for a Palestinian, other than

---

[4] See Romans 13:1–7. Scripture quotations in this chapter are from the NEB.
[5] Daniel 2:37.   [6] Daniel 2:21.

22

indifference, was narrow and extreme – either to be a paid official of the colonial administration collecting taxes for the disposal of Rome, or to join the anti-imperialist resistance party, which engaged in forays against the Roman army, ultimately leading to open war in AD 70, when the Romans destroyed the Temple in Jerusalem and suppressed those involved in a particularly brutal way. Because of the claim of Jesus to be the Messiah, there can be little doubt that He tended to attract Zealots among His disciples (such as Simon and possibly Judas and the sons of Zebedee), that He Himself was mistakenly thought to be a Zealot, and that some saw His death at the hands of the Roman authorities as the death of a Zealot leader: the inscription on His cross was 'King of the Jews'. The Zealot background to the ministry of Jesus is spelt out in more detail elsewhere in this book.[7] Suffice it to say here that it is impossible to understand fully our Lord's teaching on the State and the use of violence without taking into account the Zealots' political programme and guerilla strategy.

Yet throughout His life Jesus was careful to acknowledge the authority of the Roman administration. For the Zealots, the ultimate test of loyalty to Zionism was the payment of tax. It was on precisely this burning issue that both the Herodians, who were the collaborationists, and the Pharisees, whose sympathies lay more with the Zealots, asked him the question, 'Are we or are we not permitted to pay taxes to the Roman Emperor?' To say 'yes' unequivocally would have aligned Him with the imperial power and the henchmen of the Roman administration. To say 'no' would have identified Him as a Zealot, a determined opponent of the political power of Rome. Jesus' answer to the question was, 'Pay Caesar what is due to Caesar, and pay God what is due to God'.[8] This does not put Caesar on an equal footing with God, but is simply a recognition that within its sphere the State has a legitimate authority over its members. This same theme occurs in our Lord's trial. Pilate, feeling increasingly uneasy over

[7] See pp. 47ff., 73. [8] Mark 12:17.

the blatant miscarriage of justice which he is administering, angrily demands an answer from Jesus to a particular question, arguing, 'Surely you know that I have authority to release you, and I have authority to crucify you?' to which Jesus calmly replies, 'You would have no authority at all over me if it had not been granted you from above'.[9]

The authority of the courts and of the State is legitimized, not simply by force or by popular consensus, but by God. The demand for a utopian anarchy, the negation of authority by anyone over anyone, whether in a relatively modern institution such as the university or in society as a whole by the dismantling of the State, is in direct conflict both with the particular character of God's creation and with the consequences of the Fall. A society free of law could never exist as an idealized democracy. Self-interest is such, *regardless* of the type of human society, that any such experiment would certainly deteriorate either into some form of mob rule or else a rigid authoritarian structure. The saddest feature of most contemporary Utopias is their unending optimism regarding human nature.

This biblical emphasis on authority, however, is not simply a question of authority for authority's sake. God's insistence on His own authority, His creation of institutions such as the family and the State and His enunciation of the law are not the capricious follies of a Grand Megalomaniac. The acceptance or rejection of the family and the State as the framework for society and the regard or disregard of the Commandments as the basis for our lives has tangible consequences for both individuals and societies. God enunciates the law because life lived by its principles, within the orbit of those institutions which have divine approval, is ultimately beneficial both to individuals and to society. Similarly deviation from the law is bound to create a second best. The Christian is opposed to anarchy not simply because it is in conflict with the character of God's creation, but also for the pragmatic reason that any attempt to provide unlimited freedom is bound to have disastrous consequences. This theme is explicitly developed in

[9] John 19:10, 11.

Scripture by Paul, when he argued in his letter to the Christians at Rome that the civil authorities 'are God's agents working for your good': they are attempting to maintain an orderly society by punishing criminals.

Similarly throughout the Old Testament the injustices of contemporary societies are contrasted with the norm of the society whose legislation and practices are in accordance with God's norms. Ezekiel, addressing the leaders of the nation, instructs them to 'Put an end to lawlessness and robbery; maintain law and justice'.[1] Amos instructs Israel, 'Hate evil and love good; enthrone justice in the courts'.[2] What is this justice? The equality of all before the law; respect by the law for the individual as well as his property and family; impartial execution of the law; punishment for dishonest practices such as fraud, corruption and the victimization of the innocent, and proper regard for widows and orphans who were the poor of that society.

The biblical intention, then, is a society which respects the individual and the family, which has an honest judiciary and which produces tangible benefits for society as a whole. It is surely more than coincidence that the two most anti-God societies of the twentieth century, Stalinist Russia and Nazi Germany, both paid little attention to the sanctity of life, slaughtered groups within their societies for purely pragmatic and selfish reasons, attempted, although mercifully only on a small scale, to abolish the family, and flagrantly discriminated against minority groups, causing wholesale torture, suffering and death previously unknown in history.

Whose law? What order?

Emphasis on obedience to the civil authorities is one facet of the Christian approach to law and order. But equally important is the emphasis on justice. Whose law and what order are we trying to protect? Throughout Scripture we find this continual tension. Authority is of God. And yet authority is so easily abused by man. The case to support

[1] Ezekiel 45:9.   [2] Amos 5:15.

law and order can become a call to maintain the *status quo*, to support injustice and to enforce discrimination. Authority can become an end in itself.

This awareness of the abuse of authority leads biblical writers to place limits on the extent of the State's authority. We are to render unto Caesar that which is Caesar's. But only on the assumption that we can render to God what is God's. Caesar has a legitimate authority, but it is nevertheless a restricted authority. In the record of the early church, the reaction of the Jewish leaders to the success of the post-Pentecost teaching of Peter and John was to order that they stop all public speaking and teaching in the name of Jesus. In court, the reply of Peter and John was, 'Is it right in God's eyes for us to obey you rather than God?'[3] Shortly after, they were hauled up before the full Senate of the Israelite nation on precisely the same charge, to which Peter's only reply was, 'We must obey God rather than men'.[4]

Similarly in the reign of Darius the Mede, we find the competent administrator Daniel the victim of a palace plot. Because of his obvious ability, the only way his detractors could find to present him in an unfavourable light to the king was to enact a law forbidding the worship of any God or man other than King Darius. Daniel had no option other than outright disobedience. Both the early church and Daniel recognized the legitimate authority of the State. But when the State denies the right to render to God what is God's, its authority becomes illegitimate.

We find this same problem dealt with in the Revelation of John. The same Roman State which is described by Paul as being ordained of God and an instrument in God's service is here presented as a satanic monster, described with all the Old Testament imagery of contemporary apocalyptic literature as a beast with ten horns each replete with diadem, having seven heads each blasphemously named, similar in appearance to a leopard, yet having feet like a bear and the mouth of a lion. The whole world, astonished, follows the monster chanting their servile

[3] Acts 4:19. [4] Acts 5:29.

26

worship, 'Who is like the Beast? Who can fight against it?'[5] Was there ever a more inspired description of the mass idolatry of a Nero, a Hitler or a Stalin? Anyone who refuses to worship the beast is killed. Assisting the monster is another beast, apparently a lamb, but who, when he opens his mouth to speak, reveals himself to be a dragon. His function is to make society worship the horrific monster by outright delusion. This is propaganda, revealed for what it always is, persuasion based on lies. The Empire at this time had sunk to such a low level that it relied on popular support by providing subsidized food and free entertainment. For a society such as this, John advocates resistance, not obedience. The State has arrogated to itself the prerogative of God, the right to be worshipped. One can only render to Caesar by refusing to render to God.

In addition to this refusal to accept the demands of the State regardless of what it asks, a Christian has a clear responsibility, however he does it, to denounce both individual and civil injustice wherever he finds it. Paul instructs us to pursue integrity and justice. Jesus Himself first upholds the man who is gentle in spirit, who hungers and thirsts to see right prevail, whose heart is pure, who shows mercy, who is the peacemaker and who knows his need of God, and then goes on to compare his function in society to that of salt and light.

The denouncing of social injustice is seen most clearly, however, in the writings of the prophets. Essentially the prophets were outsiders in their societies, intent on describing and analysing their societies in specifically religious terms. Without exception we find them outspoken on the social injustices of their times.

They denounced the very real exploitation of the poor by the rich, and especially the deprived orphans and widows:

> 'They grow rich and grand,
>   bloated and rancorous;
>   their thoughts are all of evil,
>   and they refuse to do justice,

the claims of the orphan they do not put right
nor do they grant justice to the poor.'[6]

'Shame on the man who builds his house by unjust means
and completes its roof-chambers by fraud,
making his countrymen work without payment,
giving them no wage for their labour!'[7]

Amos, a sheep farmer of Tekoa, is particularly outspoken about Israel:

'. . . they sell the innocent for silver
and the destitute for a pair of shoes.
They grind the heads of the poor into the earth
and thrust the humble out of their way.'[8]

Isaiah says:

'Your very rulers are rebels, confederate with thieves;
every man of them loves a bribe
and itches for a gift;
they do not give the orphan his rights,
and the widow's cause never comes before them.'[9]

They were never afraid to denounce a corrupt judiciary which was using the law for their own gain:

'You that turn justice upside down
and bring righteousness to the ground,
you that hate a man who brings the wrongdoer to court
and loathe him who speaks the whole truth:
. . . you levy taxes on the poor
and extort a tribute of grain from them.'

'You who persecute the guiltless, hold men to ransom
and thrust the destitute out of court.'

'You have turned into venom the process of law
and justice itself into poison.'[1]

The prophet Micah accused the ruling élite of making justice hateful and wresting it from its straight course. Their dishonesty was the false scales, the bag of light weights, the infamous false measure, the accursed short

[6] Jeremiah 5:27, 28.   [7] Jeremiah 22:13.   [8] Amos 2:6, 7.
[9] Isaiah 1:23.   [1] Amos 5:7, 10, 11, 12; 6:12.

bushel.[2] The processes of law were being thwarted by the corruption of the judges.[3]

Habakkuk writes in similar vein:

> 'Devastation and violence confront me;
> strife breaks out, discord raises its head,
> and so law grows effete;
> justice does not come forth victorious;
> for the wicked outwit the righteous,
> and so justice comes out perverted.'[4]

With Isaiah it is a recurring theme:

> 'Shame on you! you who make unjust laws
> and publish burdensome decrees,
> depriving the poor of justice,
> robbing the weakest of my people of their rights,
> despoiling the widow and plundering the orphan.'[5]

They also exposed the violence of their societies. Ezekiel, indicting Jerusalem for departing from God, describes his society:

> 'The doom is here ... injustice buds, insolence blossoms, violence shoots up into injustice and wickedness.'

> 'The land is full of bloodshed and the city full of violence.'[6]

The words of God to the restored theocracy are:

> 'Put an end to lawlessness and robbery; maintain law and justice; relieve my people and stop your evictions.'[7]

In Amos, the people are told to

> 'Hate evil and love good;
> enthrone justice in the courts.'[8]

When Jonah had a proclamation of national repentance established in Nineveh it was that 'every man abandon his wicked ways and his habitual violence'.[9]

---

[2] See Micah 6:10, 11. [3] Micah 7:2, 3. [4] Habakkuk 1:3, 4.
[5] Isaiah 10:1, 2. [6] Ezekiel 7:10, 11, 23. [7] Ezekiel 45:9.
[8] Amos 5:15. [9] Jonah 3:8.

The prophet Micah chastised Israel:

> 'Your rich men are steeped in violence,
>   your townsmen are all liars,
>   and their tongues frame deceit.'[1]

Although separated by time and living in different societies, the prophets nevertheless present exactly the same sequence of events: a society rejects God and His law; invariably there is dishonesty, disregard for individual justice, a prostitution of the judicial process, increased insecurity for the ordinary citizen, the exploitation of the weakest groups such as widows and orphans, and an increasing resort to violence, so that the ruling élite's avaricious aims are realized both within and outside the society.

Conclusion

The Christian, then, with the radical dissenter, must find himself to some degree dissatisfied with the social system of which he is a part; imperfect man cannot but create an imperfect society. He must at times protest against specific injustices with the same sensitivity and yet outspokenness which characterized the prophets. But when he does so, he does not share the 'optimism' of the Marxist or anarchist with whom he may find himself aligned. He realizes that the machinery of government, imperfect though it may be, is not in essence an evil institution, but one given by God to provide a framework within which self-interested men can co-operate together and form a society.

It is the realistic analysis the Christian has of the state of man which enables him to see the need for greater justice in society, while at the same time upholding law and order as a necessity in a fallen world. It is a balance which is rarely held. But if our Christianity is to be related to the society in which we live, then it is vital that, as individuals, we do all that we can to maintain such a balance and always be ready to justify it to others.

[1] Micah 6:12.

2 Reform or Revolution?
Frederick Catherwood

Our age is wrongly labelled the age of permissiveness. We are supposed to be living in a time of tolerance: yet never has there been so much violent protest against other people's beliefs and activities.

Ours is an age when, in the West at least, the old beliefs which held society together have gone, and no new and commonly accepted belief has taken their place. This is a dangerous state for a free society, for freedom requires a society which disciplines itself. A self-disciplined society requires an agreed basis of belief, an agreed authority to which to appeal.

Christianity can establish that authority – it has done so in the past. Humanism, which is the only visible alternative, cannot do so. Quite apart from whether it is true or not, humanism has no grass-roots support. The humanist who tells the working man that racial discrimination is wrong is written off as a 'so-and-so intellectual' and told what to go and do with himself. Yet humanism is now beginning to take over from the Christian faith as the intellectual system on which the establishment relies as the basis for ideas and laws for running society.

But to change the basis of belief without carrying the country is to head straight for trouble, to oppose the liberal establishment against the rednecks, the protestors against the skinheads. The only reason humanism has got so far is that Christians have lost their nerve. So often they have opted out of the major issues which face society. They have been afraid to oppose the humanist with a well thought-out and solidly established Christian point of view. In so far as they have any public position at all, they have been content to reflect as inoffensively as possible whatever happens to be the current tide of intellectual opinion. As a result the average person is like a sheep without a shepherd. Hardly any of the major issues of humanist reform have enjoyed popular support, let alone been carried in response to popular opinion. Some of the changes may have been right, some were undoubtedly wrong; but the majority of people have been left behind. This is to leave the way open for the demagogue – and there is more than one about.

The protest movement – as opposed to normal reform movements – is an attempt to widen the base of intellectual ideals, or at least to give them a front of popular support. But the protest movement also does not carry the average member of the population with it. Protest is an assertion rather than an argument, and if the average man is unconvinced, the situation is worse than before. The liberal establishment is embarrassed and not helped.

The Christian church, on the other hand, is organized in the grass roots of society. It is organized to argue, in that the pulpit and the sermon are the centre of the Protestant service, and above all to relate men's knowledge of society as it is lived to a theory of what life should really be like. The abdication of the Christian church from its role in society is a catastrophe for both church and society.

Christian and non-Christian attitudes to social change

Of course humanism has picked up many of its ideas from Christianity, and so there are many issues on which the Christian will agree with the humanist. But there are also many points on which he will disagree. The Christian gospel gives a picture of human nature which the non-Christian will not always share. It gives an order of priorities which he will not always want to follow. Above all, the Christian will test the mood of the moment, the intellectually accepted ideas, against the eternal truths of the faith. He will not always be carried away, therefore, by the latest wave of intellectual opinion.

So the Christian cannot seek the limited objectives of the protestors regardless of everything else. He has to keep a balance. The Christian faith is a comprehensive and systematic faith. It is a total way of life where every part is balanced with every other. He cannot find quick solutions to one problem at the cost of raising half a dozen others. The Christian cannot pin his cause to a slogan – or even to a proof-text. He has to abide by a balanced doctrine of human nature and human affairs. The Christian way may be slower and less spectacular than the grand protest, but it is a good deal more certain and effective. The Christian is less concerned with the poses of protest and more concerned with their practical effect. And in the Christian way there are no short cuts, especially not the short cut of violence.

But it is not only on the issue of violence that the Christian parts company with the protest movement. Basic beliefs are involved, such as the Christian conviction that all men are sinners. The rich are sinners, but so are the poor. The right are sinners, but so are the left. The national enemies are sinners, but so are the nationalists. The oppressors are sinners, but so are the oppressed. The junta in power are sinners, but so are the revolutionaries. The anti-party group are sinners, but so is the party. This view must at least dampen the belief in revolution as a short cut to paradise. The Christian must at least hesitate to throw over society if he has the shrewd suspicion that the revolutionaries, for all their ardour and idealism out of office, will be subject to the same temptations in office, and with no greater power to resist them, than the men they have just turned out. If that is true, it is scarcely worth destroying society in the process of making the change.

But in disbelieving the starry-eyed supporters of revolution, the Christian does not have to be a complete cynic. It is, of course, possible to have a change for the better. Life would be intolerable if it were not. Without Christ human nature may not change. But human behaviour can change. This needs a change of society, not just a change of government. Governments, even autocratic governments, must all reflect, to a large extent, the societies they govern. There is a grain of truth in the maxim that a nation gets the government it deserves. An ungovernable society will certainly produce repressive governments. A corrupt society will probably produce corrupt governments. Christians who want better government will get more mileage from efforts to change society than they will from devising better schemes for seizing the radio station or kidnapping ministers.

Christian involvement in social reform

There are also Christians, however, who believe that only a change in human nature by the saving power of Christ can change human behaviour. They are neither revolutionaries nor reformers. They would wash their hands of all worldly affairs. They are in an old tradition, as old as the monasteries and convents of the dark ages. But they are not in the mainstream of Protestant tradition and, above all, they are not in the tradition of Christ Himself. He did not teach that expectation of future bliss can allow Christians to ignore present misery. He taught His followers about the life hereafter where there would be no sin and the Father's will would be done, but He also taught them to pray to the Father, 'Your will be done on earth as it is in Heaven'. He died to save men's souls from eternal death, but while He was alive He also saved their bodies from present disease and suffering. He preached to them of the bread of life which never perishes, but He would not dream of sending the crowds away when they were hungry until they had been fed with ordinary, perishable, earthly bread. He preached life eternal, but He also restored life on earth to the widow's son, the centurion's daughter and to Mary and Martha's brother Lazarus.

The teaching of the Bible, of both Old and New Testaments, is that God rules over earth as well as heaven. This is His creation and we are His creatures. The creation has been spoiled through sin. The light of His glory has been dimmed; the fruit of His work has been corrupted. But He has put His church on earth so that there should be some limit, so that His glory should not be completely blacked out nor His world utterly corrupted. Those who follow Him are to be the light of the world and the salt of the earth. We are to show to our fellow-men how the Maker intended mankind to live. Men were given the world in trust, and the Christian has been given the laws by which that trust is to be carried out.

At first sight this may seem arrogant. But it is not. The view which the Christian puts and which he tries to act out in his life is not his own view. He has no pride of authorship. The Christian view of life is passed down from a divine Author and has been acted out through a hundred generations. There is no arrogance in putting forward a view of life based on that authorship and that weight of experience. The arrogance of today lies in those who assert that in their generation alone, indeed in their fraction of a generation, lies the key to truth; that their unaided intellects and their untested assertions are sufficient for all the harsh problems of life.

What Christian, believing the truth of the Christian message, believing that the law of God is as necessary for this world as for the world to come, believing that it is the schoolmaster to lead his own generation to Christ, can be content to leave the field to the unproved philosophies which are now being put forward? It may not be a sin of commission, but it is most certainly a sin of omission. A Protestant monasticism which refuses to be involved in public affairs is not the path to a holy life. It is a breach of the second great commandment that we are to love our neighbour as ourself. To try to improve society is not worldliness but love. To wash your hands of society is not love but worldliness.

It may be argued by those with long memories that this is no more than the old social gospel, and that in abandoning the gospel of salvation for the social gospel seventy or eighty years ago the church went badly astray. And so it did. A social gospel cannot save. It is salvation by works under another name. Christians are right to be worried when the clergy cease to make spiritual care their first objective. Not only is the teaching of the flock a full-time job, but the preaching of eternal truth must be separated from shifting arguments over temporal affairs where the moral and technical arguments can be sorted out only by the expert who is also a Christian.

This involves preaching a social law, not a social gospel. Without the law, the world sees no need of the gospel. This generation will not find its way to the Christian faith if the gospel is preached without the groundwork of the law. And the law must not only be preached in church, it must be preached through the lives of Christians who have thought out its implications and live it and act it in full view of a watching world.

Others may react to a call to change society by saying that the Christian can do little in the face of overwhelming evil. Are we not told by John that 'the whole world is in the power of the evil one', and by Paul that 'evil men and impostors will go on from bad to worse'? The church itself represents only a fraction of the population. And, within the professing church, the great majority scarcely believe the Christian gospel. If you are a minority within a minority, how can you have any influence? How can a Christian living under a totalitarian régime hope to argue with the régime on Christian grounds? How can mere words move the massive power-structure of a feudal society? Even in the West, what hope has a Christian ethic in face of the shift of the intellectual to secular thought and the indifference of the vast bulk of society?

Four reasons for Christian action

1. If we believe in the sovereignty of almighty God, however, then all this is within His power. His grace, as Paul tells us, is sufficient, and His strength is made perfect in our

weakness. He does not command His followers to make futile gestures. The first reason for Christian action, therefore, may be described as a doctrinal one. The whole Bible is an account of the sovereignty of God. He brought Israel up out of Egypt. He gave His people the promised land. When they followed Him, He strengthened this little kingdom against its enemies. When they left Him, He let events take their course and they were taken into captivity. When the seventy years of captivity were over, He moved a heathen king to send them back. He enabled Nehemiah to rebuild Jerusalem in the face of hostility all around. The Christian church itself started as a few frightened men and women in a locked room.

2. If the first reason for not giving in to objections to the need for Christians to change society is doctrinal, the second is historical. Over two thousand years the Christian church and the Christian faith have had enormous influence. When it was born, the Roman Empire dominated the scene. If Christianity is a fraction of a fraction now, what was it then? The Empire was totalitarian and powerful. The ideology which was supposed to cement it together was emperor-worship, as alien to the Christians as any ideology today. Yet it was the church which survived, not the Empire. It was the belief in the deity of the emperor which faded, not the belief in the deity of Christ. The faith has had its times of peril – more peril from its professed followers once it became respectable than from Goth or Vandal, Saracen or Moor, Communist or Fascist. It has had its times of weakness, but always there has been the power of God to pull it back, to set it on course and to re-establish its vigour.

3. The third reason is practical. The Christian faith is true. It gives a true account of human nature. The Bible is the Maker's handbook. It gives the only authentic and consistent account of how men can live together in society. When it is applied it works. No other ideology can combine order and freedom. The Christian is not a quack, experimenting on society with the latest bright and untried ideas. He is the sound practitioner, to whom society

instinctively turns when the latest bout of quackery has brought it to its knees.

Of course much has passed for Christianity which is nothing of the kind. The kingdom of God, Jesus told us, is like a great tree which shelters many strange fowl. Men may have been hanged for stealing sheep in a so-called Christian country, but they were not hanged on any Christian principle. Although the laws of ancient Israel are not binding on the Christian church, it is interesting to note that they were a good deal more severe on offences against the person than on offences against property. They would certainly not have punished a train robber more severely than a murderer.

In putting forward policies for today's world which are based on Christian principles, we are not trying to push some way-out or impractical ideal. Solutions and policies put forward on Christian principles should be more practical, more balanced, freer from unforeseen side-effects than those put forward on other principles. Take one example, often seen as a niggling bone of contention – Sunday. The Christian rule of one day in seven when everyone who can takes the whole day off work is now almost universally adopted, at least in principle, even in Communist countries. And even if the onslaught on it today is substantial, the Christian can be sure of solid support from the working man; and not just for the principle of one day in seven away from work, but for one day in the week when business closes down – which is a good deal more restful than a day when you are off work but everyone else is working.

Christian views of respect for the individual are seen too in the move since the Reformation to more democratic forms of government and latterly in the free collective bargaining of Trade Unions. Though Christians may differ, individually, it is in countries strongly influenced by the Protestant ethic that democracy and free collective bargaining have taken strong root. Christian views of the material universe, which take it as a gift from God, to be held in trust and developed for the benefit of mankind, are behind the now universally accepted ideas of economic growth and development. There is no government which would now dare to admit that it had no policies of economic development for its people, no rich country which would refuse to subscribe to the development of a poorer country.

4. The fourth reason for positive Christian action is spiritual, in that it is based on the fact that God's Spirit operates to some extent in all men. Orthodox Christians have reacted strongly against the heresy which, despite all the evidence to the contrary, makes salvation universal, whatever a man's beliefs or actions. But, in his reaction, the orthodox Christian has gone too far and has tended to ignore, if not deny, the doctrine of 'common grace' that all men were made in the image of God (however marred the image might be), that men have a moral sense and an ability to be creative in their turn, in 'subduing the earth' and 'having dominion' over it. So, for instance, I know a Christian in a communist country who, when dealing with communist officials on church business, appeals to their consciences. He says, 'They are just like any other men. They all have consciences. They know in their hearts what is right and what is wrong.'

Reform or revolution?

So the Christian case for the positive reform of society is based on sound doctrinal, historical, practical and spiritual reasons. The case is that there is a need for reform in every society; that the Christian has a duty to tackle it; and that, given time and patience, Christian reform is likely to be both practical and effective.

But if the Christian is likely to be effective as a reformer, by the same token there is no need for him to be a revolutionary. The revolutionary case is not based on doctrine. The argument is the pragmatic one that reform will not work. A South American Christian once told me, 'You in Britain know nothing of the problems we face. Nothing but revolution will move things in Latin America.' But my argument is that reform by Christians on Christian principles is the only truly effective force for change. Non-Christian reform on non-Christian principles is likely to be ineffective. Contrast the history of many nineteenth-century 'liberal' movements in non-Protestant Europe with the reforms actually effected during the same century in Britain.

Revolution is also likely to be ineffective. The French have as much experience of revolution as anyone in Europe, and they have an axiom, 'Plus ça change, plus c'est la même chose'. The revolution of 1789 produced the emperor Napoleon – which was certainly not the object of the exercise. The revolution of 1848 produced another emperor, Louis Napoleon, which was certainly not the object of that exercise, either. The Russian revolution produced Stalin. The Germans threw over the Kaiser only to land themselves with Hitler.

This is not a series of coincidences. Revolution removes the landmarks of society. In a state of social chaos, when nothing holds, and when nothing and no-one can be taken for granted, those who find themselves in power have to crack down ten times as hard as they would in a stable society where there is trust between citizen and government and a social system which is largely self-policing. The force necessary for effective revolution is immensely destructive. Because it requires men to change their actions without changing their minds, everything has to be imposed by force. In the absence of self-regulation, the revolutionaries are driven to resort to terror. In the course of the terror, the hard men come out on top and if the idealists protest, they are liquidated. Then, as the saying goes, 'The revolution devours its own'.

The hard men come out on top not just because they are hard men but because society demands order. Human nature cannot tolerate prolonged chaos. People do not like the uncertainty of troubled times; they want to crawl out of the rubble, bury the bodies, light a fire, open a shop, and restore the familiar round. Whoever gives them normal life again, even at the cost of special powers for the police, will have their grudging support.

The history of revolution is a history of failed ideals. Maybe the initial objectives succeed. Maybe an unpopular ruler is toppled. That is not too difficult in some countries. But that is only the beginning. The question is whether the ideals behind the revolution come to anything. And in nine times out of ten they do not. In nine times out of ten, the backlash is more powerful than the revolution. And in the tenth case one wonders whether the ideals might not have been attained without the revolution.

There is a sense in which the Christian message is a powerful revolutionary agent. It was reported of the early Christians, 'These men have turned the world upside down'. And so they had. But though the Christian is a revolutionary in one sense, he is most strictly instructed by the apostle Paul that he must not rebel against 'the powers that be', 'for there is no authority except from God, and those that exist have been instituted by God. Therefore he who resists the authorities resists what God has appointed, and those who resist will incur judgment.'[1]

Paul goes on to give the reason: 'For rulers are not a terror to good conduct, but to bad . . . he is God's servant for your good. . . . Therefore one must be subject, not only to avoid God's wrath but also for the sake of conscience.' Paul does not define exactly what is meant by the 'authorities', the 'powers that be'. However it is clear from the passage that they are the powers which 'bear the sword' and to whom the citizens 'pay taxes'. They are the effective government of the country, the government capable of exercising justice and levying taxation. The prohibition, in other words, does not cover such minor powers as the public company, the trade union and the university. In a free society the relation of the individual with these powers is one of contract. But what seems to be absolutely prohibited to the Christian is any attempt to overthrow the recognized government. And if that was true under a tyranny, how much more true under our elected government.

---

[1] Romans 13:1, 2, RSV.

Christian arguments for revolution

Now in a revolutionary age, where the authorities are always the villains and the revolutionary always the hero, this is a hard saying. It is a tough proposition to swallow. However unsuccessful revolutions may be, when revolution is in the air the idealism of many Christians is stirred. A number of arguments are used to oppose these very plain words.

First, there is the appeal to the Protestant heroes, Coligny in France, William the Silent in Holland, Cromwell and William of Orange in England, Gustavus Adolphus in Germany, and maybe some would even wish to include that American revolutionary, George Washington. We are asked, Were all these men wrong? And what would have happened to Christian liberty without them? This is a big subject, but there are three broad answers to this proposition.

The first is that not even a Protestant hero can overthrow apostolic teaching. Indeed, as the history of Ulster shows, it is even possible to have a surfeit of Protestant heroes. Ulster might be a more Christian province if it heard less of William of Orange and more of Christian charity.

The second is that it is not at all clear that the revolutions of these heroes were all that beneficial to the Christian cause. Coligny took the sword and perished by the sword. It is possible to argue that had the Huguenots not joined the movement against the king, the monarchy would not, when it regained its strength, have revoked the edict protecting them and effectively banished them from France. William the Silent may have gained the United Provinces, but he lost the rest of the Netherlands, which then became the 'cock-pit of Europe'. It is arguable, too, that the Thirty Years War between Protestant and Catholic in Germany not only damaged Germany, but the whole cause of the Christian religion. The Protestant cause was as mixed up with the politics of the German princes as that of the Huguenots was with the French princes. Hard men were using religious feeling for their own ends and the final peace left not a triumphant Protestant cause, but a Germany sickened of religious strife. Cromwell held power for a brief decade, but as soon as he was dead, there was a violent reaction and the restored Stuart king ejected the Puritans from the churches. The Stuarts even outlasted William of Orange and died out only when Anne died without surviving children. As for George Washington's historic breach in the English-speaking nation, it is at least arguable that the world would be a better place if the breach had never taken place and that to the extent that we have ignored the breach it has been a better place. It is certainly arguable that the generation of the Great Reform Bill would have conceded what George III and Lord North refused.

Whether or not we agree with these arguments, I hope I have said enough to show that the answers to these questions are not to be found by waving the Protestant banner. But there is a third answer which gives more credit to the Protestant leaders. Each of them faced the problem of rebellion and each of them argued that they were not in fact in rebellion. The Huguenots argued in *Vindiciae contra Tyrannos* that the king of France had exceeded his constitutional powers. The Dutch argued that the acknowledged power in their country was William, the Stadtholder of Holland, and not the distant Spanish king. Cromwell argued that the British power was the king in Parliament and only in Parliament. The German princes argued their constitutional rights against those of the throne of the Holy Roman Empire. William of Orange argued that his father-in-law had abdicated in favour of his daughter, William's wife, who had asked William to share her throne. And George Washington argued that power resided in the American States and not in the Court of St James, 4,000 miles away.

So every single Protestant leader who came into conflict with an authority which might be held to be the civil power of apostolic teaching felt compelled to argue that it was not. None, because of Christian teaching, felt he was free to argue a straightforward case for a forcible change of government.

If they took note of Paul's injunctions we must at least do the same if we use them to support our case.

The other major argument used for the Christian's involvement in forcible revolution is that if the government is patently not 'God's servant for your good' then its authority falls to the ground and the Christian is no longer under any obligation to obey it. I understand that this has been Ian Paisley's reason for disobeying the Ulster government.

But the government ruling over the people to whom Paul's letter was addressed was the Imperial government of Rome, arbitrary, autocratic and corrupt and, under Nero, wildly irresponsible. Yet they were to obey it. Of course when they were asked to disobey a higher law and worship the emperor as God, or when they were ordered not to preach, they obeyed God rather then men. But they respected the Roman imperium. Paul told a runaway slave to return to his owner (though he suggested that the owner might release him for Christian service), he respected the Roman courts, he stood on his rights as a Roman citizen, he appealed from the local courts to Caesar's own court at Rome. At no point did he order the slaves to throw off the Roman yoke. At no point did Jesus Himself tell His followers to rise against Caesar. The Jews did rise and were slaughtered and dispersed. The Christians did not rise and they prevailed not by force of arms, but by force of influence and example. That surely is the Christian way: to promote peace and not war, to promote love and not violence.

Sometimes the case for the Christian to stand against Nazi tyranny is cited as an example of the rare occasion when the Christian may rebel. Hitler rose to power in a Germany in which nine people in ten attended church, and the world has been asking ever since why the German people did not stop this tyranny. But this is surely an argument against revolution and not for it. Hitler was the revolutionary, the user of force in the streets, helped, of course, by the revolutionary creed of communism which enabled him to excuse his violence as the self-appointed protector of the people against communism itself. But if the churches had been in sound condition, if their authority and self-confidence had not been weakened by absurdly exaggerated literary criticism of the Bible, if they had worked out a Christian attitude to racialism and nationalism and revolution, then Hitler would never have succeeded. He would never have picked up enough seats in the Reichstag to be appointed Chancellor. He would never have been allowed so to intimidate his opponents that he could pass the 'special laws' under duress. And, even when in power, he would never have had the political support to do the things he did. The documents now show him to be as sensitive to political support as any politician. Had the German churches been what they should have been, there would have been no need for them to be revolutionaries. As they were not, they were incapable of launching an effective revolution even if it had been right to do so. 'You are the salt of the earth; but if salt has lost its taste, how shall its saltness be restored?'[2] Certainly not by revolution.

The German Christians did not know that they were to be tested. Had they known, they would no doubt have prepared. But it is not for us to condemn them. The question is whether we are prepared for what may happen in our own generation. If we are not, then future generations may look on us as we look on the German Christians of the thirties, as the holders of eternal truth who failed to hold up that truth against the mood of the day and show where that mood would lead.

Whatever our circumstances, it is up to us to put a Christian alternative. We must take the steam out of genuine grievance by constructive reform. We must be as lights in a dark world. We must be the salt which prevents the corruption of our own society.

We must not fail. But if we are to succeed we must act, and act now.

[2] Matthew 5:13, RSV.

3 The Way of Christ[1]
Alan Kreider

The Christian's first duty

'The first duty of a revolutionary', the late Che Guevara is said to have remarked, 'is to make a revolution.' In this revolutionary age, what is the first duty of the Christian?

There is no question currently facing the church which deserves more searching consideration than this. And, in fact, it is being dealt with, in one way or another, by Christians of all parties and proclivities. In the midst of much argumentative confusion, two general groupings with markedly dissimilar attitudes to social change have emerged. On the one hand, there are radicals who are deeply disturbed by the racial discrimination, economic inequalities and social injustices which they see as symptoms of a general, world-wide malaise. Only by fundamental and often violently-induced changes can these injustices be eradicated and rightful power be given to the 'unyoung, uncoloured, unpoor'.[2] Left-wing Catholic thinkers see justification for their position in the radically egalitarian nature of the eucharist.[3] Czech Protestant theologians, though reluctant to speak of the 'just war', now unblush-

[1] This chapter owes much to the ideas, and the unpublished writings, of Dr John H. Yoder. It originally appeared in somewhat altered form in *Christian Graduate,* March 1969.
[2] The title of a notable example of this approach: Colin Morris, *Unyoung, Uncoloured, Unpoor* (Epworth Press, London, 1969; Abingdon Press, New York, 1970).
[3] Brian Wicker, *First the Political Kingdom* (Sheed and Ward, London, 1967), pp. 81 ff.

ingly advocate the 'just revolution'.[4] American theologians of the new stripe have seen revolutionary action as an integral part of the Christian's mission in ushering the world into a secularized kingdom of God.[5]

The reactionaries, on the other hand, view the *status quo* of Western society, with its forms of government, distribution of wealth and social inequalities, as God-given and good. In this conviction leading evangelicals, hotly condemning the covetousness and false prophecy of those who think that the church should have anything to do with revolution,[6] join hands with Latin American Catholic bishops. And most church members, oblivious of the theorizing of the radicals and the dogmatizing of the reactionaries, remain solidly and stolidly conservative, calcified in thought and deed.

Must the church, one is forced to ask, be left with these two violently antagonistic camps? Is there no alternative position which can combine genuine and effective compassion for the downtrodden with scepticism about the fruits of violence? It is the purpose of this chapter to suggest such an alternative.

Jesus and the option of violence

It is often forgotten that Jesus Christ was born into a climate that was every bit as revolutionary as that of Bolivia or Venezuela today.[7] The Palestine of the first century was

[4] Prague Peace Conference, 'The Just Revolution', *Frontier,* Spring 1967.
[5] For example, see Richard Shaull, 'Revolution: Heritage and Contemporary Option' in Carl Oglesby and Richard Shaull, *Containment and Change* (Collier-Macmillan, London, and Macmillan, New York, 1967).
[6] Dr Billy Graham's sermon 'False Prophets in the Church' states this position with force and eloquence (*Christianity Today,* 19 January 1968, pp. 3–5).
[7] Information which is indispensable to an understanding of the background to Christ's ministry is provided in Oscar Cullmann, *The State in the New Testament* (SCM Press, London, 1957; Scribner, New York, 1966), chapters 1 and 2; S. G. F. Brandon, *Jesus and the Zealots* (Manchester University Press, 1967), chapter 2; and W. R. Farmer, *Maccabees, Zealots, and Josephus* (Columbia University Press, New York, 1956; Oxford University Press, London, 1957).

an occupied country, restively submitting to a none-too-benevolent Roman rule. The Romans tampered outrageously with Jewish religious practices, and the very fact of their hegemony wounded Jewish pride. Small wonder, therefore, that the Jews should have looked forward to a military deliverer who would expel the Romans and re-establish God-fearing rule in Zion. The instrument of this vindication they identified with the long awaited Messiah, and the messianic expectation was exceedingly lively in the Palestine of Jesus' day. The form which it took, however, owed as much to the apocalyptic and apocryphal literature of the period between the Testaments as it did to the Old Testament Scriptures – possibly more. Such books as 1 Enoch (especially chapters 37–71) and the Apocalypse of Ezra stimulated a hope for an earthly messianic kingdom centred in Jerusalem and encouraged the idea that it would be ushered in by force. Those parts of the Old Testament message which spoke not only of judgment but of the peaceful transformation of society (*e.g.* Isaiah 2:3, 4) and included the Gentiles among those who would share in the blessings of the messianic age were all too easily overlooked.

The pious Jew of the first century, therefore, might well have found it difficult to distinguish between the nationalistic and spiritual elements in his messianic hope. Were they not a nation chosen by God to be His own peculiar people and to whom He had given the land of Canaan as their own special possession? So in the minds of many, including the fiercely pious guerilla fighters, the Zealots, who sought to deliver their fellow countrymen from the occupying armies of Rome, the national and spiritual strands of their messianic hope were inextricably intertwined.

It was these Zealots who, in the time of Christ, were the leading claimants to the messianic role. And throughout the years between their founding in AD 6 and the final obliteration of Jewish national existence after the Bar Kochba revolt of AD 135, Zealot sentiment smouldered ominously, on occasion being fanned into such flaming deeds of heroism as the insurrection which was finally

48

quelled with the capture of Masada in AD 71. Our leading source for the history of the Zealots is the Palestinian Jewish historian Josephus, who comments extensively (and in somewhat jaundiced fashion) about them in his *History of the Jewish War against the Romans* and his *Antiquities of the Jews.* We also learn about the extent of Zealot activities from various biblical passages. To choose a few random examples, Gamaliel, in Acts 5, recites a whole catalogue of fake messiahs. (It is interesting to note that he considers Jesus to be a candidate for inclusion in this category.) Barabbas is described by Mark (15:7) as a man 'who had committed murder in the insurrection'. And in Acts 21:38 there is reference to an Egyptian Jew who had been put to death by Felix for having caused an insurrection of 4,000 Zealots.

Recent writings, based in part upon archaeological discoveries and the study of the Dead Sea Scrolls, have enabled us to be more sympathetic to the Zealots than was previously possible.[8] No longer do we need to follow Josephus in categorizing them all as unprincipled and self-seeking brigands devoted primarily to wreck and mayhem. Instead, we can now see them for what they were – pious Jews, passionately dedicated to the law and fanatically adherent to a faith which would permit 'No king but Yahweh'. It is therefore understandable that they opposed Roman rule and all forms of Jewish collaborationism with such bitterness and violence. For them there could be no paying of taxes to Caesar, no association with the 'Quisling' publicans. For them the nationalistic and theological causes were one and the same. At any moment God might intervene in history and anoint a Messiah who would bring salvation to His people Israel. And the Zealot must be prepared to use violent means to assist the Lord in ushering in this fondly-expected event.

On one point, at least, the Zealots were right. This revolutionary situation, in which plotting and violence were endemic, *was* 'the fullness of time' into which His Son,

---

[8] See especially the works of S. G. F. Brandon and W. R. Farmer cited above.

the Messiah, came. Let us see how Jesus' behaviour and teaching related to the political tensions of His time, for it is only in the light of these tensions that the revolutionary nature of His life and teaching may be understood.

The New Testament narratives make it abundantly clear that Christ was forced again and again to come face to face with the alternative of revolutionary violence.[9] The symbolically-stated temptation with which the devil sought at the start of Christ's ministry to deflect Him from His calling was to recur often in highly concrete form. Recent scholarship has suggested that up to five of Jesus' twelve disciples had Zealot connections.[1] Repeatedly the disciples demonstrated their inability to think of their Teacher's mission except in terms of militant nationalistic messiahship as traditionally conceived. Peter's confession of Christ was followed almost immediately by his attempt to dissuade his Master from the road of suffering. The sons of Zebedee could think of the kingdom of God solely in earthly terms in which they might sit in court beside their king. The disciples' argument in the upper room may be thought of as an attempt to establish a hierarchy of influence in a messianic privy council. When Peter finally denied his Master, it was only after it was clear that no messianic result such as he had hoped for was to be expected from Jesus.

The expectations of the crowds exerted a similar pressure on Jesus. At various points their enthusiasm had decided political overtones, as in John 6:15 where they attempted to make Him king. W. R. Farmer has shown that the use of the palm branches in Jesus' triumphal entry into Jerusalem referred to the Maccabean resistance movement.[2] Jesus accepted this, and proceeded to cleanse the Temple in messianic style. Finally, in Gethsemane the alternative of revolutionary violence must still have been before Christ. He must have thought of His disciples, two of whom were

[9] O. Cullmann, *The State in the New Testament,* chapter 1, is especially lucid on this point.
[1] *Ibid.,* pp. 14–17.
[2] W. R. Farmer, 'The Palm Branches in John 12:13', *Journal of Theological Studies,* 1952, pp. 62 ff., cited by O. Cullmann, *op. cit.,* p. 38 n.

armed. He must have remembered the city which had wel-comed Him as Messiah only a few days before. He had the assurance of the support of twelve legions of angels. Thus we can see that Christ's ministry from the first to last represented a constant encounter with the option of revolutionary violence.

Yet Jesus resisted this temptation. He rebuked the devil for suggesting that He be a political Messiah. He performed the remarkable feat of getting ex-publicans and ex-Zealots to co-exist in one disciple band. He condemned as specifi-cally satanic Peter's suggestion that He should not suffer. When the crowds became over-enthusiastic in the wrong cause, He again and again withdrew from their midst. And in Gethsemane He remained true to the messianic calling as He alone understood it. He was obedient unto death, the agonizing death on a cross.

So Jesus decisively rejected the Zealot alternative in practice. But did He also do so in theory, in His teaching?

Some of Christ's teachings make sense only when placed against a background of Zealotism.[3] Consider the famous 'Render unto Caesar' passage, for example.[4] Some Pharisees and Herodians, attempting to 'entrap him in his talk', tried to force Jesus into an openly partisan position, either as a Zealot or as a collaborator. Jesus' answer was masterly, and got Him out of a shrewdly-laid trap. Yet it nevertheless contains the kernel of His whole attitude to the State. To it certain things should be given, such as the coins that it issues, even if they bear the inscription of a divinity-claim-ing emperor. But to God are to be given those things that are God's: one's life, one's ultimate loyalty. Jesus thus accepted the State, but with an all-important proviso. Neither the Zealots nor the collaborationists could claim Him as one of their own.

Consider also the injunction, delivered to His disciples in the Sermon on the Mount, 'Do not resist one who is evil'. Or again, consider the baffling passage in John 10:

[3] For this argument, and most of the documentation which buttres-ses it, see O. Cullmann, *op. cit.,* chapter 1.
[4] Matthew 22:15–22; Mark 12:13–17; Luke 20:19–26.

'All who came before me are thieves and robbers.' To whom was He referring? John the Baptist and the prophets are generally spoken of as the forbears of Christ, yet these could hardly have been meant here. It is far more likely that He was referring to the Zealots, who caused widespread bloodshed in their theocratic causes.

Finally, we should note Jesus' reluctance, evident in all the Synoptic Gospels, to appropriate to Himself the title Messiah. He silenced the demons who confessed Him. He commanded the disciples not to spread the identity which Peter's confession had revealed. Even at His trial, He avoided an open claim to the title. When asked whether He was the Messiah, He replied invariably, 'You say that I am.'[5] Yet when He spoke of Himself, He called Himself the Son of man, a term with less inflammatory connotation than that of Messiah.

The result of all this is clear. Throughout His ministry Jesus was confronted by the Zealot alternative of violence which must have been especially attractive because it fitted in with the messianic notions which were prevalent at the time. Though tempted by these ideas, He rejected them decisively.[6] Instead He brought to His contemporaries a new vision of the role of the Messiah, an amalgam of

[5] O. Cullmann, *The Christology of the New Testament* (SCM Press, London, and Westminster Press, Philadelphia, 1959), pp. 117 ff.

[6] S. G. F. Brandon, in a learnedly-argued and meticulously-documented book, has contended that 'there seems to be nothing in the principles of Zealotism . . . that we have definite evidence for knowing that Jesus would have repudiated' (*Jesus and the Zealots*, p. 355). (Brandon presents his arguments in capsule form in 'Jesus and the Zealots', in F. L. Cross (editor), *Studia Evangelica*, IV, Berlin, 1968.) Evangelicals, who affirm the inerrancy of Scripture, will *a priori* find it impossible to accept a position which is based on the assumption that Mark, writing just after the collapse of the Jewish national resistance (after AD 71), fabricated the figure of the pacifist Christ in order to protect Roman Christians from an aroused Roman populace (*Jesus and the Zealots*, chapter 5). And, quite apart from the scriptural evidence cited in the text above and by O. Cullmann, *The State in the New Testament*, pp. 19–23, there are at least two other reasons to doubt the validity of Brandon's position. In the first place, whereas the Zealots indignantly condemned all association with evil-doers and collaborationists, Jesus, according to all four Gospel writers, repeatedly scandalized pious Jewish opinion by fraternizing with tax-collectors and sinners. If it is significant that several of Jesus' disciples

Isaiah 53 and the Son of man passages from Daniel 8.[7] The incarnate God-man was to be a servant rather than a conqueror. The Romans failed to recognize this, and perforce they executed Him as a Zealot.[8] Yet He was not a Zealot. He was in fact arrested by the Romans precisely because He was unwilling to act like a Zealot. He was obedient unto death to a higher calling.

What ethical conclusions can we draw from this which will be of help in a revolutionary world? First of all, if we accept that Jesus is God's revelation of Himself, His final pronouncement in exemplary form on how men should live, we are forced to take the actions of the historical Jesus as the key to the Christian position on the State and revolution. His behaviour in politically-charged circumstances becomes ethically normative for His disciples who find themselves in similar situations. It is a command constantly reiterated in the New Testament that Christ's disciples are to model themselves on their Master. Christ is represented as living within His disciples. We are enjoined to have the mind which was in Christ Jesus. We are to be 'conformed to the image' of Christ. We who say we abide in Him 'ought to walk in the same way in which he walked'.[9]

What does this mean? It means, to put it bluntly, the cross. We are not only to believe in Him: we are to suffer for His sake. Christ repeatedly told His disciples to take up their cross and follow Him. He did not use the term 'cross' in the sweetly pious sense which has become fashionable. The cross to Christ was not some unavoidable form of

had Zealot connections, certainly it is equally striking that one of them had been a publican (see William Klassen, 'Jesus and the Zealot Option', *Canadian Journal of Theology*, XVI, 1970, pp. 16–17). Secondly, it is inconceivable that Mark, writing less than 40 years after the death of Christ, could have dealt so violently with the oral traditions of the church as Brandon suggests. There were, after all, other sources which were used by Matthew, Luke and John, and these sources dovetail remarkably with the Markan narrative.

[7] O. Cullmann, *The Christology of the New Testament*, p. 161.

[8] On this point see O. Cullmann (*The State in the New Testament*, chapter 2) and S. G. F. Brandon (*Jesus and the Zealots*, chapter 1).

[9] Galatians 2:20; Philippians 2:5; Romans 8:29; 1 John 2:6. Scripture quotations in this chapter are from the RSV.

suffering, such as an impacted wisdom-tooth. Rather, Christ used the term to refer to suffering which could be avoided but which was freely accepted in view of the larger benefit which would result from it. This was what the cross was to Christ personally, for He need not have died. But He chose to give His life that we might live. And we who call ourselves disciples are to imitate our Master. Our ethical norms are to be set, not by society, not by the law (which is merely a lowest common denominator necessary for the relatively frictionless co-existence of sinful man), not by our neighbours, but by Christ Himself. We are to be revolutionary – as He was revolutionary.

Secondly, we are faced by the fact that Jesus established a new type of community which, when true to its calling, is far more revolutionary than anything envisaged by the Zealots, or by Che Guevara for that matter. To this new society Christ has, by example, by teaching, by the indwelling of the Holy Spirit, given a new way to live. It has a new way of dealing with offenders, by forgiving them; with money, by sharing it; with social classes, by making them irrelevant; with racial differences, by making men of all colours brethren in Christ; with the State, by respecting it, obeying it so long as it commands nothing contrary to His way, by denying it the clerical blessing it so much desires, by praying for it. He has taught it a new way of dealing with enemy nations, by loving them, seeking to help them, blessing them rather than cursing. And He has given His new society a new way of dealing with the problems of society in a revolutionary world – by serving men rather than by seeking to be served.

The church is to be the servant of mankind. Nowhere is this more forcibly expressed in the Scriptures than in Luke 22:24-27. Jesus' disciples, still thinking in conventional messianic terms about an earthly kingdom, are in the upper room debating about their comparative greatness. Jesus, however, rebukes them:

> 'The kings of the Gentiles exercise lordship over them; and those in authority over them are called benefactors. But not so with you; rather let the greatest among you become

as the youngest, and the leader as one who serves. For which is the greater, one who sits at table, or one who serves? Is it not the one who sits at table? But I am among you as one who serves.'

The Gospels record two commissions which Christ left to His new society: the missionary commission, to preach the gospel to all nations; and the commission of compassion, to serve the needy of the world. For as we can see in Matthew 25:31–46, it is in our needy brother or neighbour that our love for God Himself will be expressed and tested. This new society thus has a revolutionary programme of action. It is revolutionary, not in the sense that it will threaten to topple Empires, but that it will offer men a totally new type of life which has wide-ranging social consequences.

The creation of 'Christendom'

But what has this revolutionary society, this community of redeemed men, this church become? We shall find that it has gradually turned, first, into a mirror image of a 'christianized' society, and then into a bastion of conservatism within a secular society. Instead of attempting to remain obedient to their Saviour, Christians have chosen to compromise with society in the attempt to 'christianize' it.

The result has been 'Christendom', in which vaguely Christian ideas have suffused the entire society without changing it essentially, without making it more Christ-like. In broadest outlines, let us look at the first centuries AD to see how this process took place, and then let us examine its effects in one particular area.

For the first two or two-and-a-half centuries of its existence, the church retained its identity as a living community of believers, visible as over against the non-believing world. But imperceptibly at first, and then extremely rapidly, its character changed. This can be seen most notably following the battle of Milvian Bridge, AD 312, when the emperor-claimant Constantine saw a cross in the sky and claimed it as his insignia for conquest. After he won out over his seven counter-claimants, he offered Christianity official toleration for the first time in its history. Many Christians were only too glad to accept the respite from persecution which this offered them. Soon the Christian faith was the official religion of the Empire. The church, in this 'christianized' Empire, ceased as a whole to be a body of believers committed to total obedience to their Saviour; it became instead an institution which provided the total population with religious resources.

As a result, the whole basis for ethical decision underwent a radical change. For the early church, the question of ethics hinged upon the example and teaching of its Lord. Revelation, rather than prudential calculation, was fundamental.

This was possible in a minority group. But once the church came to envelop the whole of society, and once the force of persecution was brought to bear on those who would not fit into a christianized mould, once people were converted – if nominally – in droves, the nature of ethical decision-making changed. Ethics came to be based less on the revelation of God incarnate than upon an estimation of what would work for a whole society. The right became what, if everyone would do it, would work. Effectiveness and universality became the ethical criteria. And those to whom obedience still mattered were shunted off into monasteries where they could be pious and good without shaking up the rest of 'christianized' society, without disturbing 'business as usual'.

Pacifism and the church

Let me illustrate this transformation by choosing one area of ethical choice which changed radically during the first four centuries following the death of Christ – the attitude towards Christian participation in warfare. In some circles today there is debate concerning the proper Christian teaching on this matter. Recent scholarship by Professor Roland Bainton, however, has shown that there was little doubt about the matter in the early church.[1] Up to the decade of the 170s AD there are neither surviving writings by Christian authors on the subject nor examples of Christians serving in the Roman armies.[2] But it is certain that the former is to be explained by the fact that the matter was not subject to controversy: abstention was simply taken for granted. Said Celsus, the pagan critic of Christianity, in that decade: 'If all men were to do the same as you, there would be nothing to prevent the king from being left in utter solitude and desertion, and the forces of the Empire would fall into the hands of the wildest and most lawless barbarians.' This objection, so typical of post-Constantinian Christian thought, did not as yet strike the Christians as relevant. The Christians were not the whole of society; and furthermore, Christ, not expediency, was their ethical model.

The position of the early Christian church on war was based not so much on specific biblical texts, although they of course cited these, as upon the mind of Christ as they understood it. Arnobius, writing sometime between 304 and 310, assumed that the tranquillity of the Pax Romana was the result of the peaceableness of the Christians. 'For since we in such numbers have learned from the precepts and laws of Christ not to repay evil with evil, to endure injury rather than to inflict it, to shed our own blood rather than to stain our hands and consciences with the blood of another, the ungrateful world now long owes to Christ this blessing that savage ferocity has been softened and hostile hands have refrained from the blood of a kindred creature.' Other Christians showed the supra-national concern of the early church. 'If you enrol as one of God's people,' wrote

[1] See Roland H. Bainton, *Christian Attitudes toward War and Peace* (Abingdon Press, Nashville, 1960; Hodder and Stoughton, London, 1961), chapter 5, which is a summary of the same author's article on 'The Early Church and War', *Harvard Theological Review*, xxxix, 1946, pp. 189–212. Fundamentally in agreement with Bainton is Hans Freiherr von Campenhausen, 'Der Kriegsdienst der Christen in der Kirche des Altertums', *Offener Horizont* (Jaspers Festschrift, Munich, 1953), pp. 255–264.
[2] R. H. Bainton, *op. cit.*, p. 67. The following account, including the citation from the church fathers, is based on this book.

Clement of Alexandria to the heathen, 'heaven is your country and God your law-giver. And what are His laws? Thou shalt not kill. . . . Thou shalt love thy neighbour as thyself. To him that strikes thee on one cheek, turn also the other.' Tertullian spoke to this issue with his usual forcefulness. Love of enemies he called the 'principal precept'. The Christian would rather be killed than kill, for 'Christ in disarming Peter ungirt every soldier'.

If we move from the level of theory to that of practice, we find that, from the late second century on, the virtually complete pacifism of the early church was gradually being diluted, as the numbers of Christians in the armed forces of the Empire slowly increased. One finds this most notably on the eastern borders of the Empire (Syria) and most rarely in Asia Minor. In AD 250 occurs the first recorded martyrdom of a Christian soldier. Tertullian informs us that many Christians withdrew from the army upon conversion. Some would serve in the legions in peace time, when the army had largely police functions to perform, and would withdraw in time of war. So practice diverged slightly from theory, although at most the number of Christian soldiers must have been quite small. And it is a fact that Christocentric pacifism was maintained by literally every known Christian writer up to the Constantinian revolution of the fourth century.

Even before Constantine, however, changes were gradually taking place which foreshadowed the shape of things to come.[8] Symbolic of this was Paul of Samosata, who in Palmyra in 278 became the first Christian bishop to hold the post of Civil Magistrate and to employ a bodyguard. After the battle of Milvian Bridge, things changed even more rapidly, if still gradually. It took twenty years of bloody civil war in which Christianity was an issue for Constantine to defeat his rival claimants. When he finally won out, he was acclaimed as the Lord's anointed. In the popular mind a fusion was taking place between the Empire and Christianity. Constantine ranged himself with the

[8] R. H. Bainton, *op. cit.,* chapter 6, chronicles the demise of the early church's Christocentric pacifism.

martyrs by styling himself victor; what they had commenced with their blood, he had completed with his sword. And Christians, in their joy to see the return of civil order, tended to forget that their earlier ethical stance was disappearing. By the fifth century the non-military tradition was being carried on only among the monks, who accepted Celsus' position that Christians should either accept full political responsibilities or give up having families. The double ethic, which early Christianity had scrupulously avoided, now made its entry into the church. For the majority, universality and effectiveness as prudentially conceived became the ethical criteria; for the minority, there was left only a hyper-legalistic obedience which led to self-chastisement in the desert. The early Christian solution, which had maintained the discipline of obedience within society, had disappeared. It had been replaced by a christianized society whose basic operating principles bore but small resemblance to the teachings of the Lord to whom it paid lip-service.

If this is what happened to the ethics of the church, what happened to it as an institution? As the religious equivalent of the political Empire, the church rapidly lost its role of critic of society and leaven within it. Admittedly, the political equivalents of the international and the national churches have changed with the centuries. At the Reformation, part of the international church split off into churches of nations, cities or petty principalities. The notion that the church should be equivalent to society was not questioned, except by some Anabaptists. In the centuries since the Reformation, an increasing number of people have come to see – whether by conscience or by force of circumstance – that the old equivalence of church and State no longer works. But many still speak as if it does. We are told that England and the United States are 'Christian nations'; *ipso facto* their causes internationally are those of Christ and the church. This type of reasoning leads to curious anomalies. World War I, for example, was defended by German Protestants and English Protestants, by German Catholics and French Catholics, as a just war in which all

Christians (*i.e.* all citizens) had a Christian duty to participate. The West in Korea was fighting God's fight, just as the Americans are today in Vietnam.[4] God's cause and the self-interest of nations are still all too easily confused.[5]

Not only have churches confused their identity with national entities; they have tended to break down still further into groups which serve primarily certain social classes. The nineteenth-century Church of England was unkindly labelled 'the Tory party at prayer'. Methodism was often seen as a church of mill-owners. Although these descriptions were vituperative rather than analytical, they nevertheless contained more than a kernel of truth. Churches have been and are tied to social classes, and, despite the heroic efforts of a few concerned men in many churches, the working-classes remain largely unchurched.

As though it were not enough for the churches to become yoked to nations and classes, they have also become inextricably entangled with certain economic systems. Capitalism is often presented by American evangelicals as being a uniquely Christian economic system. Christians in communist countries, on the other hand, have often claimed a divine sanction for their own brands of socialism. Is it too much, in this post-Christian era, to step back from all these Constantinian pretensions, to assert that Christ is Lord and Judge of all nations, all social classes and all economic systems?

Instead of being a consecratedly obedient and irresistibly attractive minority, most churches have been socially conservative, buttresses of a *status quo* no matter how unjust. They have sided with oppressors. They have dispensed half a

[4] As I write this, an American evangelist is busily organizing a 'March to Victory' rally in Washington, D.C., which Air Marshal Ky, as a result of vigorous arm-twisting by the Nixon administration, has regretfully decided not to attend.

[5] Malcolm Muggeridge has noted this in typically acerbic fashion in his *Jesus Rediscovered* (Fontana, London, and Doubleday, New York, 1969), p. 142. Writing of the Church of England, he has asserted that 'In the various wars of our time the Church has been insistent that God was on our side, and has given its unqualified blessing to whatever methods of waging them the generals and politicians might consider expedient'. Of how many churches in Christendom might the same statement truthfully have been written!

gospel, often unconsciously to act as a sedative, an opiate. They have been blind to need. The churches were slow to speak out against and to ameliorate the conditions in the new industrial cities of the last century, the conditions which provided the matrix in which Marxism sprang into life. They have accorded divine sanction to wars which now look ridiculous to all, pacifists and non-pacifists alike. Of course, there have been prophetic exceptions, but they have not been sufficient to outweigh the impression given by the majority of Christians. Marx, Gandhi, many Victorian intellectuals and a whole host of young people throughout the world today have rejected and are rejecting the church on moral grounds. The church has not only been found to be indifferent to social injustice; it has rightly been seen as an integral part of the whole problem.

Think of the impact of the 'Christian West' on Vietnam. An evangelist or cleric goes to Vietnam and baptizes the war effort as God's fight. For all the people there can tell, Christianity is being preached and the war is being waged by the same people. This *mésalliance* is proving to be a serious impediment to the propagation of the gospel in that country and throughout the developing world, as a Vietnamese student evangelist recently discovered. 'Christianity', a neighbour taunted jeeringly, 'is part of the USA's plan to take over our country.'[6] The Constantinian synthesis has thus led the church into a terrible impasse. How shall it extricate itself?

Revolutionary Christians

There are Christians, most notably in Eastern Europe and South America, who attempt to do this by siding with the revolutionary forces in the world. They are bitterly critical of the past and present yoking of Christianity with the West. With this one can fully agree. Many of them point out that in current history God is very probably at work in revolutionary movements throughout the world. Again one

[6] James K. Stauffer, 'Vietnam is Dying', *Missionary Messenger*, December 1967, p. 5.

is forced to agree. One needs only to recall the use that God made of Cyrus and Nebuchadnezzar to realize that He may be using unexpected instruments today to bring about His purposes in the world. Yet when these Christians go beyond this to assert that, since God is working through revolutionary movements, it is the church's task to rush in uncritically to build socialist Utopias, one is forced to disagree vigorously. To them the church is still subservient to a secular social order; God is still on 'our side'; and the church is criticized, not for having confused its identity with a given social order or nation, but simply for having backed an obsolete ally.

What then should the Christian be saying about revolution? He should begin by surveying, in as calm and analytical a manner as possible, the fruits of past revolutions. And as he does so, he will be driven to the conclusions that there is no certainty in the method of violent revolution, and that revolutions have seldom managed to produce more than a shadow of their promised results.

He will come to these conclusions, in the first place, because it is obvious that the revolutionary process is exceedingly difficult for any individual or group to control coherently. Situations of revolutionary violence seemingly have internal motive forces of their own, forces which transcend the individuals involved in them, which compel the revolutions to go through a natural sequence of stages (which almost inevitably end in some type of reaction),[7] and which ruthlessly discard the leaders of each stage as 'the refuse that will be swept into the dust-bin of history'.[8] Thus, in revolution after revolution, the moderates who guided the early stages of revolutionary activity have been superseded by radicals. And the radicals, in their turn, have

[7] Two such 'stage theories' of revolution, which have much in common with each other, are provided by Rex D. Hopper, 'The Revolutionary Process', *Social Forces*, xxviii, 1950, pp. 270–279, and by Crane Brinton, *The Anatomy of Revolution* (W. W. Norton, New York, 1938; George Allen and Unwin, London, 1939).

[8] The phrase, so reminiscent of the verbiage of America's current Vice-President, is Leon Trotsky's. See Crane Brinton *et al.*, *A History of Civilization* (Prentice-Hall, New York, and Bailey Bros. and Swinfen, London, 1955), ii, p. 476.

also been discarded in favour of relatively conservative, traditionalist forces. For example, in the French Revolution, a Mirabeau led inexorably to a Robespierre, who was after a short period of power forced to give way to the Directors. Ten years later France was ruled by an emperor, Napoleon I. Twenty years later another Bourbon was on the throne. Similarly, in the Russian Revolution the moderate socialist Kerensky was forced to yield the reins of power to Lenin and Trotsky who, through death and deportation, were also forced to surrender the machinery of State to that twentieth-century equivalent of Ivan the Terrible, Joseph Stalin. Even in the Chinese Revolution we see a similar force at work, with the exclusion of such 'enemies of the people' as Liu Shao Ch'i and the emergence of Mao Tse-Tung (or his well-cultivated image) as a modern counterpart to the Mandarins of old.

In the second place, the Christian looking analytically at the revolutions of the past will observe that the cost of the revolutionary method is forbiddingly high. It is perhaps a relatively minor matter that large amounts of property are destroyed in the course of revolutions, either by the revolutionaries or by their opponents. But it is more serious that successive purges, such as the Terror of 1793-94 in France or the Stalinist treason trials of the mid-1930s, brought about the liquidation, often on dubious pretexts, of group after group of conservative *and* revolutionary leadership. Most alarming of all, however, are the baleful consequences of revolutionary violence on the populace at large.[9] For who can measure the cost in human lives of the liquidation of the Russian *kulaks* or the decimation of the Indonesian Chinese population following the recent revolution *manquée* there?

The pragmatic non-Christian might conclude that purgative blood-letting such as this might be tolerable in view of the glorious society which might thereby be achieved. The careful Christian analyst, however, is forced to note, in the

[9] Peter L. Berger makes this point eloquently in his contribution to P. L. Berger and R. J. Neuhaus, *Movement and Revolution* (Anchor Books, Doubleday, New York, 1970), p. 56.

third place, that there is real doubt whether many violent revolutions have changed anything fundamental in the societies that they have purportedly revolutionized. The Puritan programme to enforce public morality in the 1640s and 1650s, for example, led directly to the libidinous excesses of Restoration England. The French Revolution succeeded in converting *les malheureux* of the eighteenth century into *les miserables* of the following century.[1] The secret police of Stalin's Russia differed from their Czarist predecessors chiefly in their greater efficiency, while a 'New Class' of well-paid bureaucrats replaced the exiled and decimated aristocracy at the pinnacle of the 'classless' social pyramid.[2] George Orwell, in *Animal Farm*, brilliantly exposed this failure of the revolutionary method to change society fundamentally. And, with the mordant wit of those who are resigned to their fate, an eastern European recently commented that the only difference that he could see between capitalism and communism was that, whereas under capitalism man exploited man, under communism the opposite was the case!

The Christian should not be surprised at these pessimistic conclusions about the fruits of the revolution. For when he moves from an analysis of the past to an examination of basic Christian presuppositions, the Christian will realize why revolutions produce less than they promise. He will see furthermore that the problem of the violent revolutions is not that they are too radical but that they are not radical enough. It is not that they change too much, but that they change too little. For revolutionary Utopias are based on an over-optimistic estimate of human goodness and perfectibility. They are based on the assumption that humans may

[1] Hannah Arendt, *On Revolution* (Viking Press, New York, 1965), p. 110.
[2] On this controversial point, see the perceptive comments of Milovan Djilas, *The New Class: An Analysis of the Communist System* (Thames and Hudson, London, and Praeger, New York, 1957), chapter 3. See also Alf Edeen, 'The Civil Service: Its Composition and Status', in Cyril E. Black (editor), *The Transformation of Russian Society* (Harvard University Press, 1967), pp. 285 ff., and the more general observations of H. R. Trevor-Roper, 'The Past and the Present', *Past and Present*, 42 (1969), pp. 6–7.

be coerced into virtue. They are the result of attempts to fight violent societies with violent means.

But the disciple of Christ knows that Satan cannot drive out Satan. He knows that those who take the sword shall perish by the sword. He knows that only those who are without sin are in a position to throw stones, and that not a single human is without sin. He knows that only those who have first removed the planks from their own eyes can remove the specks from the eyes of others. The Christian knows, in other words, that means are integrally involved in ends, that sin, rather than merely being a culturally-conditioned phenomenon, is universal to the human race.[3] And, because of these insights, he will recognize as terribly superficial any attempt to end oppression by exterminating an oppressor class. He will be sceptical of revolutionary promises. He will be capable of seeing the obvious fact that socialist Utopias have not changed the nature of man. And he will seek to make his contributions to the amelioration of the human condition not after the model of Chairman Mao but after that of Jesus Christ.

For the Christian faith, when working with full power, revolutionizes men. It converts them, not in a narrowly pietistic sense, but as whole men. If genuine, this conversion effects a radical departure from normal human reactions and attitudes. Love and altruism replace greed and self-aggrandizement as the mainsprings of human endeavour. The follower of Christ, modelling himself on his Master, will attempt to respond to insult and ignominy with suffering love. He will overcome evil with good. The Christian, therefore, cannot blithely say that rich men, as representatives of the old social order, may be bumped off; rather he will seek to make the rich into self-giving disciples of his Master. Loving concern for the enemy is a fundamental ingredient of Christianity. This involves love for the extortioner, the petty dictator, the over-brutal policeman, the reactionary bishop. There is no place in the Christian's life for hatred, even of oppressors. In a situation

[3] Biblical passages alluded to in this paragraph are: Matthew 12:26; 26:52; John 8:7; 1 John 1:8; Matthew 7:5; Romans 3:23.

of conflict, the Christian's prime concern is for the enemy. He prays for his persecutors; and he leaves vengeance to God. Accepting the fact that all social orders are less than just, the Christian will attempt to ameliorate them and make them more human. But he will do so in the way of Christ. This may involve righteous anger and moral force. He dare not, however, wittingly inflict permanent harm on anyone.

The relevance of the church

What relevance, then, can Christians, collectively knit together in the church, have in this revolutionary world? First of all, the Christian church should be communities of men and women engaged in demonstrative action. The practical manifestations of the Spirit of Christ – complete brotherhood, genuine mutual love and concern, selflessness – should serve as a sign or parable to an unbelieving generation. Of the early church it was said, 'How they love each other!' Can that be said of the church today? Can it, like the early church, absorb hostile groupings into a new entity which transcends them? If we cannot love our brother, though he be of another social class or another colour, what chance have we of loving our enemy? But if we can be a truly supra-national, inter-national, inter-racial amalgam of all social classes, we shall be a sign, a demonstration of the living power of God that this disorientated world cannot fail to recognize.

Second, the church must work as a self-giving body. The prime call to it must not be that of wealth, or of security, or of comfort; above these must be placed God's call to give a cup of water in His name to His needy children. The great gulf between the rich nations and the poor nations, and between the affluent and the deprived classes at home, must therefore be a matter of intense concern to Christians. As Barbara Ward has said, 'Christians straddle the whole spectrum of rich nations, and therefore Christians are a lobby, or can be a lobby, of incomprehensible importance in this field. If we don't do it, when we come to see God ultimately, he will say: "Did you feed them, did you give them a drink, did you clothe them, did you shelter them?" If we say: "Sorry, Lord, but we did give 0.3 per cent of our gross national product", I don't think it will be enough.'[4]

Self-giving will thus involve Christians in more than making generous deposits in the collection boxes on Sunday morning; it will involve them in political action, for by their political pressure Christians, if properly mobilized, can influence governments to allocate tax money to help those people and nations who most need assistance. This will entail social involvement as well. Christians should gravitate towards those professions which directly meet the needs of the under-privileged. In addition, they should seek to practise their professions in the places where the need is the greatest. Human need rather than personal preference or prudential calculation must be the basis of Christian vocational choice.

Third, the church must serve as a reconciling body. The hatred between antagonistic nations, races and classes is intense. The alienation of man from his neighbour may seem quite impossible to bridge, yet it is the calling of Christians to be ministers of reconciliation.[5] Christians must strive to end wars. They must do all they can to ameliorate conditions under which wars are fought, not only by giving generously from a distance but by being good Samaritans on the spot. They must provide food for the hungry and clothes for the naked, not because this may aid some 'pacification' programme, but perhaps in spite of it. They will do this because it is the way they can help their neighbour in distress. And in helping their neighbour they will serve Christ. Domestically as well the Christians should be where tensions are most intense. Christians must meet the racial problem head on. This cannot be done by pious statements by church leaders, nor by occasional expeditionary forces of whites into predominantly Negro areas. It

[4] David L. Edwards (editor), *Christians in a New World* (SCM Press, London, 1966), p. 27.
[5] 2 Corinthians 5:18.

must be done by Christians who are residents, by Christians who are willing to be neighbours of their black brethren in a physical as well as a theological sense.

Christians must not flee revolutionary situations, for their very presence in these situations may be one of the few rays of hope in an otherwise inextricably violent situation. As Richard Shaull has pointed out, 'Any hope for a significant Christian contribution to the revolutionary struggles going on around the world will depend . . . on the emergence of new forms of Christian community on the front lines of revolution. Such groups can have no pretension of being political movements; they need make no claims to special authority, nor exclude anyone interested in their objectives. But they can offer the context for a continual running conversation between our theological and ethical heritage and the major human issues that arise in the attempt to transform society. It is just possible that in such weak and informal communities new ideas and questions may take shape which will be of significance for the revolutionary movement as a whole. . . .'[6] In such situations, pacifist Christians can do things which other Christians cannot do. They will not only be known as men of honesty and concern who care for the welfare of all, but will be able, as they have been able in the Kenya Mau-Mau uprisings, the tense eastern Europe of post-war days, and the contemporary tragedy of Vietnam, to keep open channels of contact which may some day lead to reconciliation.[7]

Fourth, and finally, the church must serve as a prophetic body. Colossians 2:15 informs us that Christ has triumphed over the rebellious principalities and powers.[8] Although they remain ordained for man's good because of his sin,

[6] This sane observation, along with much that is more objectionable, occurs in Oglesby and Shaull, *op. cit.*, p. 247.

[7] See Hans de Boer, *The Bridge is Love* (Marshall, Morgan and Scott, London, and Eerdmans, Grand Rapids, 1958), *passim*, and John Miller, *No Cloak, No Dagger* (East-West Relations Committee, Society of Friends, London, 1965), especially chapter 1.

[8] See H. Berkhof, *Christus en de Machten* (Callenbach, 1953), available in North America as *Christ and the Powers*, trans. John H. Yoder (Herald Press, Scottdale, Pa., 1962); O. Cullmann, *The State in the New Testament*, pp. 66–70.

they have lost their absolute claims. It is the church's job to resist the powers when they become rebellious, and to remind them of their limited authorization for man's good. When they assume absolute powers, or when they command action which is contrary to the will of God, they must be defied. The church must not allow itself to be swallowed up in nationalistic fervour. As a prophetic body, it must maintain its independence, perspective and obedience, despite the fact that this will inevitably mean remaining a minority group.

Thus, in sum, it is the first duty of the Christian church, in this revolutionary age, to be the church. Instead of establishing revolutionary cadres, pietistic communities, or big prosperous churches, Christ calls the church to be the sacrificial society which He established to be the servant of mankind. It is to preach a gospel which meets the need of the whole man. It is to love friend and foe alike, limitlessly, without counting the cost. It is to be revolutionary as Christ was revolutionary. If it fulfils its calling, Christians will certainly be rewarded at the last with the comforting words:

> 'Come, O blessed of my Father, inherit the kingdom prepared for you from the foundation of the world; for I was hungry and you gave me food, . . . a stranger and you welcomed me, I was naked and you clothed me, I was sick and you visited me, I was in prison and you came to me.'[9]

May it be so with us.

[9] Matthew 25:34-36.

4 Revolution and Revelation
René Padilla

There is a whole range of possible definitions of the term
'revolution'. The one consecrated by general use in school
textbooks · is that which makes reference to social and
political events 'clearly different from all other phenomena
because they suddenly cause a violent and far-reaching
change in the whole pattern of society and especially in the
traditional political structure that is being transformed and
replaced by a new order'.[1]

For the Christian as an individual and for the church as a
community, such events create an ethical problem that
demands an answer. What position should they take?
Isolation? Participation?

The position that we take obviously depends, among
other factors, on our political ideas. We must not deceive
ourselves about our objectivity; it is even possible to use
theology to justify attitudes whose roots are not in revelation, as we would like to think, but in purely human
premises. If we reject revolution, it may be that our rejection is due, more than anything else, to a compromise with
the *status quo* and a fear that change might affect our own
economic position. If we support revolution, on the other
hand, it may be that our support is due to the fact that we
have been conditioned by the myth of man's ability to build

[1] Arend Th. van Leeuwen, *Desarrollo y Revolución* (Editorial 'La
Aurora', Buenos Aires, 1967), pp. 36 f.

a new world order. For this reason it is urgent that we place our motive under the judgment of the revelation of God in His Word.

This must be the starting-point of our theological consideration of revolution. Its purpose must be to clarify the significance of our commitment to Jesus Christ in relation to today's revolutionary ferment, to understand the mission that Christian discipleship involves in the midst of the conflicts and the political, social and economic changes that surround us. All this should result in a fuller, more integrated Christian life.

Revolutionary ferment in the Bible

Every revolution is characterized by a certain ambiguity which makes it difficult to evaluate from a Christian point of view. It would be much easier to decide for or against a revolution if all the factors involved were always perfectly clear and definable. The problem is that usually they are not. In every revolution there is a mixture of good and evil, light and darkness, white and black.

On the positive side, revolution presupposes the recognition that life in society is not what it ought to be, that it is deformed by evils that demand a radical change in the social structures. The revolutionary is, at least on the surface, a nonconformist *par excellence*. His very existence depends on the premise that something is wrong with the world – so wrong that whatever action taken to remedy the situation cannot be limited to mere reformation of the present order. What is required is a new order, a world purged of all the weeds, the abuses and the imperfections that alienate man. This is the world that he seeks to bring in by means of revolution.

The Christian cannot close his eyes to the injustices that surround him. To do so would be to deny an important aspect of the Hebrew-Christian tradition. Seven centuries before Jesus Christ, Amos, the shepherd from Tekoa, proclaimed the judgment of God against those who exploit the poor:

O you who turn justice to wormwood,
and cast down righteousness to the earth! . . .
They hate him who reproves in the gate,
and they abhor him who speaks the truth.
Therefore because you trample upon the poor
and take from him exactions of wheat,
you have built houses of hewn stone,
but you shall not dwell in them;
you have planted pleasant vineyards,
but you shall not drink their wine.
For I know how many are your transgressions,
and how great are your sins –
you who afflict the righteous, who take a bribe,
and turn aside the needy in the gate.
Therefore he who is prudent will keep silent in such a time;
for it is an evil time.[2]

The same courageous denunciation of the abuses of the rich is found in the messages of other prophets of Israel: Isaiah,[3] Micah,[4] Jeremiah,[5] and Ezekiel.[6] One of the greatest glories of the Jewish people is that from them arose the first champions of social justice.

This prophetic note breaks into the world of the first century in the preaching of John the Baptist.

'You brood of vipers! Who warned you to flee from the wrath to come? Bear fruits that befit repentance, and do not begin to say to yourselves, "We have Abraham as our father"; for I tell you, God is able from these stones to raise up children to Abraham. Even now the axe is laid to the root of the trees; every tree therefore that does not bear good fruit is cut down and thrown into the fire.'[7]

Asked about what conduct is fitting in the light of the judgment of God, John answers, 'He who has two coats, let him share with him who has none; and he who has food, let him do likewise'; tax collectors ought not to charge 'more than is appointed' and soldiers should not take advantage of their position to become rich by extortion.[8]

Jesus Christ Himself defines His mission in words of profound social significance when He says,

[2] Amos 5: 7, 10–13. Scripture quotations in this chapter are from the RSV.
[3] Isaiah 1:16 f., 23; 3:14 f.
[4] Micah 2:1 f., 8–11; 3:9–11; 6:9–12; 7:3. [5] Jeremiah 2:34; 22:3.
[6] Ezekiel 22:29. [7] Luke 3:7–9. [8] Luke 3:11–14.

'The Spirit of the Lord is upon me,
because he has anointed me to preach good
    news to the poor.
He has sent me to proclaim release
    to the captives
and recovering of sight to the blind,
to set at liberty those who are oppressed,
to proclaim the acceptable year of the Lord.'

His whole ministry is marked by a constant identification
with the destitute – an identification that won Him the
title 'Friend of tax collectors and sinners'. The crowds
move Him to compassion because they are 'like sheep
without a shepherd'. He chooses His disciples from among
the common people, the *am-ha-arets*, scorned for their
ignorance of the law. He teaches that no-one can serve
God and wealth, He cautions against the deceitfulness of
riches, He warns the rich that their comfort in this world
will be limited to their material possessions, and He accuses
those who in the name of religion exploit widows.[9]

In the actions and words of Jesus there is a revolutionary
ferment that, apparently at least, corroborates the Jewish
leaders' accusations against Him before the Roman authorities – that He is subverting the order. Although the thesis
that Jesus was a Zealot cannot be sustained on the basis of
biblical data, it must be recognized that there is a grain of
truth in it – that Jesus shares with the Zealots their dissatisfaction with the established powers and their hope for
the coming of the kingdom of God.

This prophetic tradition finds echo later in the teaching
of James:

'Come now, you rich, weep and howl for the miseries that
are coming upon you. Your riches have rotted and your
garments are moth-eaten. Your gold and silver have rusted,
and their rust will be evidence against you and will eat
your flesh like fire. You have laid up treasure for the last
days. Behold, the wages of the labourers who mowed
your fields, which you kept back by fraud, cry out; and the
cries of the harvesters have reached the ears of the Lord of
hosts. You have lived on the earth in luxury and in pleas-

[9] Luke 4:18–19; Luke 7:34; Mark 6:34; Matthew 6:24; Mark
4:19; Luke 6:24; Matthew 23:14.

ure; you have fattened your hearts in a day of slaughter. You have condemned, you have killed the righteous man; he does not resist you.'[1]

Revolution and human nature

So the Christian stands in a prophetic tradition. He agrees with the revolutionary in his desire for a better world where justice and liberty reign. Biblical faith does not permit the Christian to be resigned to the *status quo* nor to align himself with the oppressor. However, this same faith demands that he has reservations about the dynamic of the change proposed by the revolution.

Every revolutionary ideology presupposes a faith in man's ability to create a new world. It sees the historical process as the result of factors over which man has control. Obviously, not *any* man, but only the revolutionary. In a sick society, plagued by the evils of misery and exploitation, the revolutionary represents the only hope for a new order, because he, and only he, is free of contamination by the régime in power. 'Because of the historic possibility that it glimpses ahead of it, the revolutionary group (class or nation) considers itself a messianic group, the principal protagonist of history, for the period that its action initiates, and which is the final period.'[2] Underlying this messianic sense is the conviction that man is good by nature, that evil is not inherent in man, but only in the social structures that condition him. The immediate objective of the revolutionary, therefore, is orientated toward changing these structures. And it is in order to accomplish this objective that he resorts to violence. Violence thus becomes the moving force of history, the way to usher in the perfect society.

The Christian agrees with the revolutionary in his dissatisfaction with the state of things as they are and the desire for a change in the situation. He admits with the revolutionary that what is needed is not only technological and industrial development, but a complete change, a

[1] James 5:1-6.
[2] Georges Marie-Martin Cottier, 'Muerte de las ideologias?', *Criterio*, LXIII, 1569 (10 April, 1969), p. 204.

transformation of the whole system. He disagrees with the revolutionary, nevertheless, in that he does not believe in violence as *the* solution for social problems, *the* road that leads to the perfect society. He may perhaps recognize with Reinhold Niebuhr that there may be occasions when the balance of power, necessary for justice, demands violence as the comparatively lesser evil.[3] That would be the case in a 'borderline situation' in which the Christian would accept violence and at the same time the blame and the necessity of God's forgiveness which violence implies.[4] What simply does not fit into the mental system of the Christian is violence as the norm of history.

The Christian's rejection of violence is consistent with his understanding of man and society. The unjust conditions that prevail in society are not brought about primarily by causes outside man. They are, rather, the result of the inclination toward evil that is inherent in man. This is basically a *moral* question. It finds its centre in the very essence of man. In the words of Jesus Christ, '*From within, out of the heart of man*', come all these evil things which defile man.[5] In the final analysis, here is the root of all social evils. 'This is the centre of the ills of humanity – the I out of place,' says E. Stanley Jones.[6] And he adds, 'Everything else is a symptom – this is the disease.' Quacks try to cure the symptoms; doctors cure the disease.

All human history corroborates this analysis. There has always been an element that has eluded the examinations of politicians, sociologists and economists, but which has

[3] R. Niebuhr, *An Interpretation of Christian Ethics* (Meridian Books, New York, 1956; Mayflower Books, London, 1957), pp. 170 ff.

[4] Helmut Thielicke has rightly emphasized the guilt of the Christian who is forced by circumstances to follow a course of action opposed to the law of God. 'In such extreme cases,' he writes, 'untruth cannot be regarded as a "commanded" way of escape, for if we regard it as commanded, what we have is again an evasion of the conflict situation, and this is always wrong. It is rather that in such cases a man is prepared to accept the guilt of untruth.... He is willing to take this guilt upon himself, not in the name of the tragics, but in the name of forgiveness.' H. Thielicke, *Theological Ethics*, Vol. 1, *Foundations* (Fortress Press, Philadelphia, 1966), p. 662.

[5] Mark 7:21–23.

[6] E. Stanley Jones, *La Victoria Personal* (Abingdon Press, Nashville, 1966), p. 20. Only the Spanish translation was available to the author.

determined to a large extent the course of historical events – the moral corruption of man, human depravity, what theology calls *sin*. Every interpretation of history that ignores this element will necessarily be idealistic. If there is anything that history teaches us, says Herbert Butterfield, it is that human nature cannot be trusted: 'It is essential not to have faith in human nature. Such faith is a recent heresy and a very disastrous one.'[7]

Like the revolutionary, the Christian desires the destruction of all the patterns of the established order that enslave man. He echoes the words of the prophet, 'Let justice roll down like waters, and righteousness like an ever-flowing stream.'[8] But, following Jesus Christ, he knows what is in man.[9] Furthermore, he sees in history the judgment that falls upon those who try to transform society before transforming the individual, that 'law of gravity' which pulls down to earth man's dreams of building a new world for himself. For this reason, he discounts 'the' revolutionary solution and looks for a revolution that is still more radical, more complete, a revolution that will overcome the estrangement between man and God and between man and his neighbour. As Nicholas Berdyaeff has said, 'The Christian is the eternal revolutionary who is not satisfied with any way of life, because he seeks the kingdom of God and his righteousness, because he aspires to a more radical transformation of man, of society and of the world.'[1]

The problem with violence is not that it is radical, but rather that it is not radical enough. It attempts to eliminate the symptoms without curing the illness. It prescribes pep pills when what is needed is a surgical operation. Its error stems from an erroneous concept of man. The revolutionary closes his eyes to the moral deformity of human nature – this evil whose depth even the idealist Kant was forced to admit – and thus trusts in the adequacy of his ideology to

[7] H. Butterfield, *Christianity and History* (G. Bell, London, 1949; Scribner, New York, 1950; Fontana, London, 1958), p. 66.
[8] Amos 5:24.   [9] See John 2:25.
[1] N. Berdyaeff, *La Afirmacion Cristiana de la Realidad Social* (Casa Unida de Publicaciones, Mexico, 1936), p. 24.

establish a new order. He assumes that social evils are a question of political, social and economic organization, and that they will disappear through changes external to man. Sooner or later his ideal of a perfect society will be shipwrecked on the reef of the human ego. From this not even the revolutionary is exempt. No political party nor social class, neither the bourgeois nor the proletarian, is immune to the desire to convert itself into a god and appeal to force to achieve its own ends. Revolution does not change man; it does not touch the root of social evils. For this reason, as soon as the revolutionary régime is established the injustices of the old order reappear and the revolutionary class becomes a new oligarchy. The revolutionary becomes the defender of the *status quo* and his ideology of change becomes the *instrumentum regni*, the means of power that is transmitted to the masses on the basis of authority, thanks to a monopoly on education, literature and the mass media. As Romano Guardini has warned, man has power over many things – and today more than ever! – but he does not have power over his own power.[2]

The gospel of revolution

Every revolution sets before the Christian faith the question of the relation between the kingdom of God and the kingdoms of men, between eschatology and history. In the final analysis, every revolution is a human attempt to create here and now the perfect society that God has promised to create at the end of the present age. The problem is to know to what extent the new order introduced by the revolution is the fulfilment or (at least) the beginning of the fulfilment of the purpose of God in history.

We must begin by recognizing that nothing in the world lies outside the control of God. God rules over all the nations of the earth and He executes His government through Jesus Christ. Jesus Christ is Lord not only of the church but also of the whole creation. This is the consistent

[2] Romano Guardini, *The End of the Modern World* (Sheed and Ward London and New York, 1957), p. 109.

teaching of the New Testament.[3] Furthermore, according to the biblical record, God uses 'secular' powers that remain outside the sphere of redemption to work out his purposes for the world. In Isaiah, for example, Cyrus is described as God's anointed one, raised up 'to subdue nations before him and ungird the loins of kings'. In Romans Paul refers to the authorities as 'ministers of God'. In the presence of Pilate Jesus Christ Himself admits that the judgment being passed on Him is based on an authority that comes from God Himself.[4] Are we then to say that God is the author of violent revolutions?

This, in effect, is the thesis sustained by some contemporary theologians. To them, revolutions are nothing less than the means through which God is carrying out His purpose in history. God's action is of a political nature – it is orientated toward the transformation of social structures. Harvey Cox says that God is present above all in political events, in revolutions, in revolts, in invasions, in defeats. God not only permits or desires change, but He carries it out, and He does this through revolutions.[5] Richard Shaull, in agreement with Paul Lehmann, maintains that 'revolution must be understood theologically, for it is set firmly in the context of God's humanizing activity in history. As a political form of change, revolution represents the cutting edge of humanization.'[6] He believes that the presence and power of God in the renovation of life are manifested above all wherever there is a struggle to make human life more human, 'on the frontiers of change where the old order is passing away and the new order is coming into being in the world'.[7] In the light of this concept of revolution, the

[3] Matthew 28:18; Romans 1:5, 6; 1 Corinthians 8:6; Ephesians 1:10, 21–23; Philippians 2:9–11; Colossians 1:18.
[4] Isaiah 45:1; Romans 13:6; cf. 13:4; John 19:11.
[5] Harvey Cox, The Church amid Revolution (World Council of Churches; Association Press, New York, 1967); El Cristiano como Rebelde (Ediciones Marova, Madrid, 1968). Only the Spanish translation was available to the author.
[6] R. Shaull, 'Revolutionary Change in Theological Perspective' in John C. Bennett (editor), Christian Social Ethics in a Changing World (World Council of Churches; SCM Press, London, and Association Press, New York, 1966), p. 32.
[7] R. Shaull, 'The New Challenge before the Younger Churches' in

responsibility of the Christian is obvious – to be present in the revolution, involved in the struggle for 'humanization', though always aware of the possibility of 'dehumanization' and ready to admit the limitations of the new revolutionary order.[8] Cox concludes, 'God is acting; if we want to relate ourselves to Him, it is imperative, then, that we also should act.'[9] Shaull says, 'Our task is not to impose certain values, but rather to recognize and live according to those that hold sway in the world; it is not to give meaning to life, but rather to discover the meaning that life has in the world that participates in redemption; not to establish order in the universe, but rather to share in the new order of things that is taking shape through social transformation.'[1]

This position, which the Conference on Church and Society held in Geneva in 1966 adopted as its platform, represents above all a way of thinking characteristic of our time, particularly in underdeveloped countries – the position according to which violence offers the masses the only hope of change. Salvador de Madariaga, the Spanish writer, has observed that the West today lives in the disillusionment that belongs to a post-revolutionary stage in which it has lost faith in violence and has chosen to submit to dictatorial governments.[2] Whatever the validity of this thesis may be in regard to the West, in the rest of the world the hope generally prevails that, on the basis of a supposed dialectic of history, revolution will create the new society that the majority desires. The 'theology of revolution' takes upon itself to provide theological justification for this hope. All its errors stem from the fact that it takes as its starting-point the revolutionary situation and interprets Scripture

Edwin H. Rian (editor), *Christianity and World Revolution* (Harper, New York, 1963), p. 210.

[8] R. Shaull, 'Revolutionary Change in Theological Perspective', pp. 32 ff.

[9] Harvey Cox, *op. cit.,* p. 36.

[1] 'Y un Dios que actua y transforma la historia', *America Hoy*, Published by I.S.A.L. (=Church and Society in Latin America) (Montevideo, 1966), p. 61.

[2] *De la Angustia a la Libertad* (Editorial Sudamericana, Buenos Aires, 1966), p. 41. Another author, J. C. Hoekendijk, likewise asserts that man today is a 'rebellious conformist' but not a revolutionary. *The Church Inside Out* (Westminster Press, Philadelphia, 1966), p. 46.

on the basis of presuppositions derived from leftist ideologies. Instead of showing the relevance of revelation to revolution, it makes revolution its source of revelation. The result is a secular gospel whose dominant emphases parallel those of Marxism.

The 'theology of revolution' is in essence a new version of the 'other gospel' that Paul combatted so vigorously in the first century. Like it, it holds that man can attain the kingdom of God by means of his own works. It is basically a negation of the gospel of grace. It puts man in the place of God; and not even man as he actually exists in history, with the limitations that his sinful state place on him, but an idealized man, a mere projection of an optimism devoid of biblical content. It ignores the Bible's diagnosis of human nature and takes as its basis the simplistic thesis that evil is external to man and consequently can be eradicated through change in the social structures. Its concept of man coincides with that of Marxism, not with the Christian concept, although it pretends to be an expression of Christianity.

In the final analysis, what the 'theology of revolution' challenges is the Christian's future hope. As Michael Schmaus says, the worldly optimism reflected in utopian concepts of history is the death of the Christian hope.[3] In the New Testament, the only hope that has validity is that which is based in Jesus Christ – He is 'our hope'.[4] In this other gospel, the hope is epitomized in revolution. In the New Testament the action of God is orientated toward the creation of a new humanity in which the moral image of Jesus Christ, the New Man, will be reflected; in this other gospel, the purpose of God in history is a 'humanization' to be understood in economic terms, a 'salvation' of the social structures within history. The fact is completely ignored that the ultimate cause of the injustice that prevails in the world and creates disorder in the whole of society is in man; that this is a power that cannot be purged from the present order by means of any programme contrived by man. Because they believed this, the Old Testament

[3] M. Schmaus, *El Problema Escatológico* (Editorial Herder, Barcelona, 1964), p. 27.   [4] 1 Timothy 1:1.

prophets 'set all their hope on a new creation of the world through the power of God, and rejected, as a radical delusion, the idea that a new humanity and new conditions could be created through human reforms'.[5] Their hope is carried over into the New Testament because Jesus Christ and His apostles agree with the prophets in their diagnosis of the human situation. The 'theology of revolution' idealizes man and consequently converts the gospel into a utopian ideology that employs theological terminology but has little relation to the eschatological message of the Bible.

It must not be denied, of course, that the supporters of this type of theology see revolution not as an exclusively human effort, but as the result of 'the humanizing activity of God' in history. From this point of view Shaull, for example, argues that revolution is not an inevitable process, determined by a law of history, but rather a reciprocal action involving a challenge for change from God's side and the response of obedience from man's side.[6] Instead of solving the problem of the man-centredness that is found at the very root of this other gospel, this reference to God as the ultimate author of revolution aggravates the problems, for it assumes that a human programme has God's approval. In other words, there is a 'sanctification' of revolution, which puts God at man's service. It may well be asked if this identification of revolution with 'what God is doing in the world to humanize man' is not a fulfilment of Jesus Christ's prophetic warning regarding the proclamation of false Christs in the last days.[7]

What allows the theologians of revolution to think that revolutions are the place where the action of God intervenes in history is what Paul Ramsey has aptly called 'a mutilated Barthianism'.[8] Taking as their starting-point

[5] Walther Eichrodt, 'The Question of Property in the Light of the Testament' in Alan Richardson and W. Schweitzer (editors), *Biblical Authority for Today* (World Council of Churches; SCM Press, London, 1951; Westminster Press, Philadelphia, 1952), p. 273.

[6] R. Shaull, 'Revolutionary Change in Theological Perspective', pp. 34 ff.

[7] Matthew 24:23-25.

[8] P. Ramsey, *Who Speaks for the Church?* (Abingdon Press, Nashville, 1967), p. 77.

Karl Barth's objectification of the work of Jesus Christ, they assume that the world *has been reconciled* and that all that now is asked of men is to recognize that *they are in effect living* under the sovereign rule of Jesus Christ. But they neglect Barth's 'christocentric' ethic and interpret social transformation indiscriminately as the expression of the will of God to place all things under the feet of Christ. The net result is to make violence sacred, which eliminates any possibility of discerning the elements of evil involved in all revolutions. Furthermore, if one's starting-point is the principle that, since God has reconciled the world, revolution cannot be understood except as the expression of His redemptive purpose, it is difficult to understand why the conservative should not defend the *status quo* in the name of the same universal reconciliation. When revolution is understood as an event that originates in the will of God, the Christian becomes, as in the conservative position, a slave to the social order. In spite of all the apparent differences between the revolutionary and the conservative there is basically one essential agreement – both identify the purpose of God with the present historical situation. In the one there is a conformity with the *status quo*; in the other a conformity with the revolution. 'In the final analysis, both positions identify the will of God with the so-called permanent necessities of history.'[9]

The attitude of Jesus Christ toward the revolutionary programme of the Zealots should suffice to define a Christian attitude toward revolutionary movements today.[1]

[9] Arthur Rich, 'La Revolución como Problema Teológico', *Cuadernos Teológicos*, XVI, 61 (January-December, 1967), p. 90. The whole article is a cutting criticism of the 'theology of revolution'. Rich's warning is most timely: 'We must be careful that theological social positivism (which it is hoped has been abandoned once for all) should not be replaced by a revolutionary theological positivism that accepts revolutionary changes in history simply *because they occur*. Should this happen, we would lose the necessary critical distance in relation to the dynamic, revolutionary events of our time. This would only lead to a change from conservative conformity to "revolutionary" conformity; this is one of the great dangers of every theology of *kairos*, into which in the past more than one lawyer and admirer of early religious socialism fell.'

[1] On Jesus' attitude to the revolutionary situation and movement of

The modern idea of creating a perfect society through revolution is no less evil than the Zealot's conception of the messiah as a political leader called to establish the kingdom of God by the power of the sword. And the attitude that the disciple of Christ should take toward it cannot differ from that of his Master: 'He who does not take up his cross and follow me cannot be my disciple.'

His time, see Oscar Cullmann, *Jesus and the Revolutionaries* (Harper and Row, New York, Evanston and London, 1970). Cullmann has ably shown that Jesus took an uncompromising stand against oppression as well as against those who intended to change the situation through force.

5 The Social Impact of the Gospel
Samuel Escobar

Evangelicals and social concern

Revolution, rapid social changes, transformation: these are the things of the moment, in Latin America at least. The social pressures of the masses on the fringes of society find their interpreters in the intellectuals and students, and they cannot be silenced either by military or police forces. Political agitation finds a fertile ground for every kind of extremism. Economic and political solutions from an Anglo-Saxon background simply do not work in this explosive situation.

This hour takes evangelicals by surprise with questions for which we do not have answers, for we should have thought about them years ago. In the churches, the generation gap is clear proof that this is so, and some of our best young people are leaving in search of the answers elsewhere. Though a caricature, the following summary of the situation by a young Christian is very eloquent:

> 'In the past, they told us not to worry about changing society because what we need is to change men. New men will change society. But when the new men begin to worry about changing society, they are told not to worry, that the world has always been bad, that we await new heavens and a new earth and that this world is condemned to destruction. Why try to make it better? What's even worse is that those who teach this are the ones who enjoy all the advantages that this passing world offers, and they passionately defend them whenever they are endangered.'

There has been a tendency in the evangelical church in Latin America to identify social concern with theological liberalism or with spiritual coldness and lack of concern for evangelism. It has been an unfortunate confusion. There are sufficiently solid grounds in the teaching of the Word of God and in the history of the church to affirm emphatically that concern for the social dimension of Christian witness in the world is not an abandonment of the fundamental truths of the gospel.

On the contrary, it is to take to their logical conclusions the teachings about God, Jesus Christ, man and the world which form the basis of this gospel. So why this evangelical neglect of the social responsibility of the church?

In the first place, it can be explained historically. Most of our churches in Latin America are the result of Anglo-Saxon missions which have sprung up during this century, especially after World War I. In some cases, the theology, or rather the pietistic attitude, of these missions resulted in the concept that Christian life is completely separate from the world. The hostility of a Catholic or semi-pagan environment made this 'separation' even more acute. Thus many areas of the daily life of the believer were completely disassociated from his faith. On the other hand, his rejection of the world also meant his separation from important aspects of his national culture.

But perhaps what affected our attitude most was the polemic between fundamentalism and modernism since the turn of the century, and the rejection and failure of the 'social gospel'. Any concern for social and political issues came to be identified as an attempt to introduce a 'social gospel' and finally came to the point where lack of compassion and obedience were excused by an attitude of 'defending the faith'. As Carl Henry has pointed out, this was a corruption of the evangelical struggle for orthodoxy, a dangerous distortion of its original purpose. The fact that this attitude was a distortion can be illustrated from a quotation from the last volume of the famous collection of books 'The Fundamentals' which gave 'fundamentalism' its name. Prof. Charles Erdman wrote:

'. . . a true Gospel of grace is inseparable from a Gospel of good works. Christian doctrines and Christian duties cannot be divorced. The New Testament no more clearly defines the relation of the believer to Christ than to the members of one's family, to his neighbours in society, and to his fellow-citizens in the state. These social teachings of the Gospel need a new emphasis today by those who accept the whole Gospel, and should not be left to be interpreted and applied by those alone who deny essential Christianity. . . .

Some are quite comfortable under what they regard as orthodox preaching, even though they know their wealth has come from the watering of stocks and from wrecking railroads, and from grinding the faces of the poor. The supposed orthodoxy of such preaching is probably defective in its statements of the social teachings of the Gospels. One might be a social bandit and buccaneer and yet believe in the virgin birth and the resurrection of Christ.'[1]

So our historical background may explain our negligence; but it also demands of us a re-examination of our consciences. There is another sense in which a look at our history will help us. The social dimension of our Christian witness has receded as the church has grown. Non-evangelical observers who try to interpret our presence in Latin America have pointed out that evangelicals initially made a strong social impact.[2] They were, for example, in the vanguard of the agrarian reform in Bolivia; of medical assistance in various parts of the Andes; of the school systems of Argentina, Peru, Mexico and Cuba; of civil rights and especially religious liberty; of the fight for the rights of the Indians; and many other causes.

Certain missions had a keen interest in social work, establishing schools, for example, whose reputation and influence are now part of the educational tradition of their countries. Even missions which did not have any social interest ended up establishing service institutions brought about by the urgency of the problems they confronted. So it could be

[1] Charles R. Erdman, *The Church and Socialism* in *The Fundamentals*, Vol XII (Chicago, 1911), pp. 116, 118.
[2] See, for example, the testimonies put together by George P. Howard in *Religious Liberty in Latin America*.

said, even of the most conservative missions, that missionaries at the turn of the century showed great sensitivity to human needs. But since then it is as if the churches and denominations have concentrated their efforts on the growth of ecclesiastical machinery, shutting their eyes to the needs of the world, and neglecting compassion in a typical bourgeois fashion.

One further aspect of the social impact of the gospel which should be mentioned in connection with our background and history is the rising standard of living. Starting with the lowest strata of society the gospel has produced a social mobility upward in the course of one to two generations. So we find the son of illiterate evangelical parents reaching university level thanks to the change that Christ brought about through his father's conversion. How much have our churches been aware of this fact? And are we now going to be concerned for how the gospel works out in this and other areas? 'Much will be expected from the one who has been given much.' Are we now to fulfil our own social responsibilities to our own generation?

Many voices of authority today point out the urgency of the evangelizing mission of the church. Certainly evangelism is *one* of the church's tasks, but it is not the only one, and it does not end in proclamation. Recognizing it as the central task should not lead us to close our eyes to other urgent tasks: the teaching of 'the whole counsel of God' to help the believer's progress toward maturity in Christ; corporate worship as an expression of communion in Christ; and the cultivation of that type of relationship that makes the Christian community a visible expression of the work of the Holy Spirit in the lives of men: witness, fellowship, service. The church is more than an able proclaimer in the communication of intellectual precepts. It is the visible expression of the truth that it proclaims.

Richard Halverson underlined this vital link between the life of the church and evangelism at the World Congress on Evangelism in Berlin:

'Evangelism never seemed to be an "issue" in the New Testament. That is to say, one does not find the apostles urging, exhorting, scolding, planning and organizing for evangelistic programs. In the apostolic Church, evangelism was somehow "assumed", and it functioned without special techniques or special programs. Evangelism happened! Issuing effortlessly from the community of believers as light from the sun, it was automatic, spontaneous, continuous, contagious. . . . St. Paul does not repeatedly exhort his churches to subscribe money for the propagation of the faith; he is far more concerned to explain to them what the faith is and how they ought to practise and keep it.'

It is evident how artificial it is to teach techniques on how to communicate the message entirely apart from a primary emphasis on the Christian life and the united testimony of the Christian community. That testimony of the Christian community is not simply tossed to the wind but is given to the world in specific neighbourhoods, in specific cities, in specific social structures. It is not given to abstract men, but to men of flesh and blood who live in specific social structures, who suffer, who rejoice, who are subject to error and disillusion, who struggle and hope.

As we study the New Testament, we discover that the apostolic authors were very aware of the world in which they lived and very definite in their teaching on how to live by faith within the realities and institutions of this world. The teaching of the New Testament, when not occupied with theological exposition, is occupied to a great extent with the obligations and social relations of believers – much more so than, for example, with religious duties or the exercise of piety.[3]

But this is not only a theme of New Testament teaching generally. It is a specific result of the coming of Christ into the world, for it is He who is our pattern, and our gospel, the power and wisdom of God in us, He who through the Holy Spirit is with us here and now, in this agitated world in which we live.

---

[3] These are the conclusions of the excellent work done by E. A. Judge, *The Social Pattern of the Christian Groups in the First Century* (Tyndale Press, London, 1960).

The way of incarnation

'As the Father has sent me, even so I send you.' This is the outcome of the marvellous truth of the incarnation. God made Himself man. The Word was made flesh and lived among us. Jesus did not fulfil His mission from afar. We see Him as a child who is born and grows up, as a man who lives the lot of a member of an ill-favoured social class in a country exploited by colonialism. We are not talking about God disguised as man. John himself, who so strongly emphasizes His deity, describes to us the reality of His humanity. His redemptive task would not have been possible without this identification, this living as a man in the midst of men. Friend of publicans and sinners, He accepts them, eats with them, without trying to defend Himself against the inevitable accusations which came as a consequence. This is the Lord who sends us. And this is *how* He sends us.

Sent by Him, we are also men in the midst of men. We live in a specific society, subject to human laws, to the contingencies and unforeseen fortunes to which all our fellow-men are subject. But only too often we have to admit that we have given in to the temptation of separating ourselves from society and not identifying ourselves with it. We do not have a Protestant monastery in Latin America as yet, but the attitude of a monastery does exist. There are those who dream of forming 'evangelical neighbourhoods', or educational systems in which the sons of believers will be protected from the world from the cradle to the grave. John Stott has said:

> 'I personally believe that our failure to obey the implications of this command (As the Father sent me into the world, so send I you) is the greatest weakness of evangelical Christians in the field of evangelism today. We do not identify. We believe so strongly (and rightly) in proclamation, that we tend to proclaim our message from a distance. We sometimes appear like people who shout advice to drowning men from the safety of the seashore. We do not dive in to rescue them. We are afraid of getting wet, and indeed of greater perils than this. But Jesus Christ did not

broadcast salvation from the sky. He visited us in great
humility.'[4]

How, then, do we relate our Lord's example and command to our social responsibility?

The church as a social group

The fact that the church is the people of God does not prevent it from also being a group composed of human beings
who adopt forms of social conduct and structures related to
the environment in which they live. As a result, churches
may be converted into white congregations with a segre-
gationalist theology, or middle-class churches with bourgeois mentality and customs. They may be converted into
pressure-groups within society manipulated for political
ends. They may be converted into 'cysts', growths foreign
to the social organism in which they live, producing a
culture, a way of dress, or a pattern of recreation which are
foreign to their environment. This is the danger of con-
tinuing to be men among men. We must be conscious of it
in order to combat it. We must learn to distinguish between what is biblical and fundamental and what is only a
reflection of a social and cultural background. An emphasis
on what is essential to the calling and mission of the church
is the real corrective to this sociological conditioning; but
we must recognize that this conditioning does exist.

Identification with our own people

For the historical reasons already mentioned, the churches
in South America have frequently lived within an Anglo-
Saxon sub-culture. There is only too often in our leaders
and pastors a total ignorance of the literature, folklore and
history of Latin America. Observers have pointed out the
phenomenon of the imitation of the missionary, so that
people speak with his linguistic defects or hold slavishly to
the same opinions about economics and politics. We must
learn to be men of our own country and our own generation. I am not advocating a false nationalism, an exaggerated patriotism which makes use of the national flag as a

[4] From an address to the World Congress on Evangelism in Berlin.

cover for egoistic ambitions. We must simply be aware of the place where God has placed us here and now.

In evangelism this means that we must recognize that men and women will not necessarily understand addresses copied from Spurgeon or Moody. These great preachers were great precisely because they responded to the reality of their time. To copy their messages slavishly is to distort them, because their sermons were full of references to their own times. For the evangelist, digging into our own past and present culture is an urgent task, a real social and evangelistic responsibility. Speaking about the application of this principle to the missionary, Eugene Nida has said:

> 'The identification needed is not one of imitation but of effective participation as a member of society. To participate effectively, it is not necessary to deny one's own cultural heritage – something that is literally impossible even though one proposes to do so – but to use these cultural resources to benefit the whole community to which he belongs.'[5]

And this takes us to a deeper level of identification.

A middle-class ideology?

If we examine our Latin American social structure, we will note at once that there are certain strata that we are not reaching with the message of Jesus Christ: the aristocratic land owners, the élite industrial bourgeois, the intellectuals, organized labour, vast areas of university students and the rural masses. We are, or we rapidly become, middle-class churches with a middle-class mentality.[6] Even churches which sociologically are not middle-class have developed a middle-class mentality. Yet the middle class is not a very large sector of the population. It is the other groups or social classes which are producing change. And they are

[5] Eugene A. Nida, 'La estructura de la sociedad latinoamericana y la extension del Evangelio'. Article in *Cuadernos Teológicos*, 38, April 1961, p. 137.

[6] Two protestant groups in South America do not fall into this description: Immigrants (Lutherans, Waldensians) in certain areas, and Pentecostals. We will not go into the distinctions. One might consult the vast research done in the work *El Refugio de las Masas* by Christian Lalive D'Epinay (Ed. del Pacífico, Santiago de Chile, 1968).

precisely the ones which are not being reached by the gospel. Why?

We preach a message that calls men to repentance and to a new life in Christ. Our sermons and writings call for the drunkard to leave his alcohol, for thieves and delinquents to leave their wicked paths, for disobedient children to respect their parents. We promise the neurotics that they will find spiritual peace and the psychologically disturbed that they will find the fountain of tranquillity. But what does our message have to say to the ones who exploit the Indians, to capitalist abusers, to corrupt government officials who accept bribery, to dishonest politicians? What about the comfortable indifference in our churches toward the suffering of the masses?

'Presidential breakfasts' and meetings with authorities are popular today. Have evangelicals raised a prophetic voice at these? Are we not rather trying to gain the riches and privileges of the unrepentant hearts of the powerful, guaranteeing them that the gospel will produce workers who will not strike, students who will sing choruses instead of painting walls with slogans on the social struggle, guardians of the peace at the price of injustice? We ought not to think it strange, then, that those hearts sensitive to the pain of our people, to misery and injustice, instead of being agitated by the revolutionary message of Christ that changes even the blackest heart, should go along with almost any popular ideology. We ought not to be surprised that in certain countries so many evangelical young people have become guerrillas and do not want to have anything to do with the church. Upon whom will their blood fall?

One more example of our lack of involvement and 'incarnation' in the real world is our attitude toward the problem of population. Hunger and suffering are directly related to the terrifying growth of the population. But this is not the only cause, if we are to be honest. It is also caused by the unequal distribution of wealth and unjust social structures. Many evangelicals have begun to promote birth control as a form of social work. In my opinion this is very commendable. But it would be good to see the same enthusiasm in the combating of other causes of hunger. But we do not see them. I think the answer is simple. With birth control, it is the 'lower classes' that are affected. And we are not too disturbed if they are maltreated. But when it comes to unjust distribution of wealth or of obsolete social structures, our actions and opinions will disturb the *status quo* of the 'upper classes'. We must think back to such men as John Huss and John Wycliffe, evangelical forerunners of the Reformation. Perhaps we do not realize how much the evangelical work of these men was linked to the national movements in Bohemia and England which fought against the imperialism of their day. Why did their message take root among the masses? Because it was a gospel which was not separated from flesh and blood.

Political or social programmes?

It must be clearly understood that churches are not called upon to form a political platform or party. This is not the church's mission. The message of salvation must reach each one in his own circumstances showing him how sin affects every sphere of his life and human relations. The message should also show how personal commitment to Jesus Christ will transform each life in such a way that the effects of conversion are visible to society. From what does Jesus want to save me, and for what? This is what must be preached clearly, in straightforward, understandable language, not in the unintelligible jargon of some secret sect.

When John the Baptist preached, he asked for evidences of genuine repentance before baptism. He told his hearers to act in such a way that a change in attitude could clearly be seen. He was very definite about what each one should do. To some interested soldiers he said something that would sound very relevant to our time: 'Rob no one by violence or by false accusation, and be content with your wages.'[7] Jesus was equally concrete in His demands to those whom He called. The Epistles are also notably clear. James is

[7] Luke 3:14. Scripture quotations in this chapter are from the RSV.

very precise in his instructions to that incipient middle class to whom he directed his Epistle. How abstract our versions of the gospel sound at times!

Recently I have noticed an awakening social and political conscience in certain Argentine missionaries who went to the northern part of the country to live among the Indians in order to take them the message of Christ. They have not dedicated themselves to politics in the traditional sense of the word, but they have had to revise their thinking on civic education, to speak out boldly to the authorities, to preach against discrimination, and to start a small industry. My own congregation – in the past typically impervious to the social dimension of the gospel – has been stirred to the roots on hearing what is happening.

So if the church carries the example of Christ incarnate to its logical conclusion, it cannot do less than be very much aware of the social and political context in which those who hear the message live. It will preach a relevant message. It will cease to be a monastery, or a club of contented people, or a foreign growth, a cyst on an alien culture.

The way of the cross

'The Son of man also came not to be served but to serve, and to give his life as a ransom for many.'[8] The love of God is not known only in the incarnation of Christ, in His coming to live among men. It is seen supremely in the fact that His work here ended on the cross, in His sacrificial death on behalf of sinful man. The road of exaltation which gave to Christ His final lordship passed through humiliation and the sacrifice of the cross. There is a similar road for the disciple of Christ, for the one who is sent as Christ was sent.

'By this we know love, that he laid down his life for us; and we ought to lay down our lives for the brethren. But if anyone has the world's goods and sees his brother in need, yet closes his heart against him, how does God's love abide in him?'[9] John Stott has commented on this:

[8] Mark 10:45. [9] 1 John 3:16, 17.

94

'I know, of course, that the sinbearing death of Jesus in its atoning significance and power was absolutely and utterly unique. Yet there is a secondary sense in which we, too, are called to die for the very people we seek to serve. Not until the seed dies is the fruit borne . . . We are to be ready to lay down our lives for others, not only in martyrdom, but also in self-denying service. . . .'[1]

It is interesting how the context of the words in which Jesus defines His life as a mission of service culminating in death is a discussion of power and prestige. Some see the church as a political force, or they want to transform it into one. It is an ancient temptation and we should be on guard against it.

Political power and the spirit of service

The kingdom of Christ is not of this world. It is not a kingdom that imposes itself upon men by achieving political power. Basically, the Roman Church has done just that, yielding to the temptation of creating a 'Christian society' from above by force of political power. Latin America has a sad history of alliances between political power and religion, and there are many who suspect that behind the left wing of the 'new Catholicism' there is, once again, the old temptation of promoting a revolution in order to ride on its back.

Evangelicals also fall into the same temptation via two different routes.[2] First, there is the radical left wing of Protestantism which says that today it is not necessary to preach the gospel, that the revolution is far more important, that this is *the* Christian way today. Second, there are also those who affirm that as long as evangelicals are such a small minority, they can do very little in the social or political arena, and that this is why today we must dedicate ourselves to preaching until we become an evangelical majority – that is by the sheer number of votes. In both cases there is simply a desire for power and no action is proposed without a previous takeover of power.

[1] From the Berlin Congress address quoted above.
[2] Phillip Maury discusses what he calls 'The pietist temptation' and 'The Catholic temptation' in *Politics and Evangelism* (Doubleday, New York, 1959), chapter 2.

This same temptation has sometimes caused evangelicals to play with the extreme right wing in support of totalitarianism. In some countries the Roman Church has leftist segments that are very active, placing them in open opposition to conservative régimes, and in some cases leading to open rupture. These régimes in their desire to prove that they are 'westernized and Christian' begin to court evangelicals, sending high-ranking public officials to their services, offering certain advantages to the once disreputable Protestants. Evangelicals must not allow themselves to be caught in this type of political game. But sometimes naïvety or the desire for prestige will lead them to rejoice in such 'openings' indiscriminately. At other times, a naïve anti-communism leads them to close their eyes to misery and injustice and be suspicious of anything that speaks of change.

The pathway of Christ is the pathway of service. His death leads us both to death and to a new life.[3] The new life means a new attitude toward God and toward our fellow-men, a new way of looking at things; no longer self-centred, interested only in our own happiness, our own well-being, our own 'salvation'. We must go deeper into the total dimension of the change which Christ effects in us. Our gospel is false if it leads us to believe that after an encounter with Christ, after conversion, the property owner continues to do whatever he feels like doing with his property; the capitalist stops smoking or being an adulterer but goes on exploiting his workmen; the policeman distributes New Testaments to his prisoners but continues to apply physical or mental means of extracting their confessions; the young rebels settle down and marry and get well-paid jobs, but put their money into plush homes or even luxurious buildings for the church, complete with wall-to-wall carpeting and velvet curtains.

Christ did not come to preach an armed revolution to break down unjust structures. But He expected of His disciples a revolutionary conduct characterized by the spirit of service and sacrifice. And this is really possible, if

[3] Romans 6:1–14; Colossians 2:9–23; Galatians 2:20.

man will but permit God to change him, if he turns and puts his trust in Christ. We must not convert the gospel into a message of 'Be happy; live without worries!'

The social dimension of service

The tremendous needs of every sort today present opportunities for service in the fields of education, health, assistance for isolated areas, technical help and a thousand others. The Latin American States, for example, are in no condition to take adequate care of the growing demands of the people. What is to be our Christian reaction to these needs?

Service in the Christian sense is always sacrificial. It is not a matter of giving our leftovers. It is a matter of giving our very lives, part of ourselves, 'to be spent' in Paul's terminology. It is an intelligent giving, a service in proportion to our own potential and needs. The time has come for evangelical Christians to study the needs of their own country co-operatively and then to take stock of their resources and think how to use them to their fullest potential for service.

This sacrificial and intelligent service is part of the spiritual maturity to which we aspire. The new generation in the churches should be challenged to give themselves to a life of service, to remember that they have been given much and much is demanded of them. This means that an important part of the preparation and training of all young people for Christian living will be to expose them to the need of their own country so that they can help through the backing of their congregations, or by an informed selection of their place of employment. This service will not always be in the nature of 'social service'. It may mean work in areas often neglected by Christian people, such as the media, or journalism. But whatever the job, the important thing is that it should be a real spirit of Christian service which is the motive for going into it at all.

But what of more directly social service? Here there are two factors which must be taken into account. In the first place, we live in a much more complex society, much more populated, and radically different from the society in which Jesus and the apostles lived, or from the society of the Old Testament. Our interpretation of Scripture then must take into consideration that difference and understand what obedience to the Word means in our own context today. This means that today 'to give food to those who are hungry' is not only to give bread to a beggar, but also to introduce modern techniques for the cultivation of wheat in a primitive rural community. It means that 'to give a cup of water' can mean installing an Artesian well or an irrigation system in a jungle town of Brazil. This also means that in the Bible we do not have the specific answers to the complex problems of an industrial or pre-industrial society such as ours. Part of Christian service may be precisely to explore the possibilities that technology and science are placing at our disposal. To place technical progress into the hands of the needy is a form of Christian service itself.

In the second place, it is fundamental to recognize that society is more than just the sum of a number of individuals. It is naïve to affirm that all that is needed is new men in order to have a new society. Certainly every man should do whatever he is able to do to get the transforming message of Christ to his fellow-citizens. But it is also true that it is precisely these new men who sometimes need to transform the structures of society so that there may be less injustice, less opportunity for man to do evil to man, for exploitation. The fight against slavery, for example, in which evangelical Christians played a notable part, included on the one hand an evangelistic activity that transformed slave owners, teaching them the principle that all men are equal according to the Bible; but it also included, on the other hand, the intelligent political action of an evangelical group in the British Parliament for some twenty years.[4]

Christian service also implies, then, activities whose goal is to influence the condition and behaviour of men by

[4] Regarding the work of the evangelical abolitionists and in general evangelical social action in the British world, one might consult two valuable works: Earle E. Cairns, *Saints and Society* (Moody Press, Chicago, 1960) and Kathleen Heasman, *Evangelicals in Action* (Geoffrey Bles, London, 1962).

structuring their way of life, from the conscientious vote of a well-informed citizen to participation in political and social action.[5] The specifically evangelical contribution is the spirit of service in which this active participation is offered. Latin American politics needs a good dose of that spirit. When circumstances demand it, intelligent participation could require revolutionary action in politics. If the word or the idea seem repugnant and surprising, we should ask ourselves, what position would evangelicals have taken in our battles for independence? Which one of us would have preferred the colonial *status quo*?

Service and evangelism

Service is not evangelism. Men, regardless of their social class, their economic condition or their political stripe, need to know that God loves them and that Christ offers them the way back to God. Rich and poor, capitalists and proletarians, military men and politicians need to hear the call to repentance and faith. The announcement of this good news by preaching, personal testimony, literature and other means is something which will always be the responsibility here and now of every believer. But he who evangelizes has a life that is different from others. He is one who has learned to serve. He is a 'living letter' which demonstrates the truth and relevance of the message which he proclaims. We cannot separate the proclamation of the gospel from the demonstration of that gospel. Although different, both are indispensable.

Christian service is not optional. It is not something we can do if we want to. It is the mark of the new life. 'You will know them by their fruits.' 'If you love me, you will keep my commandments.'[6] If we are in Christ, we have the Spirit of service of Christ. So to discuss whether we should evangelize or promote social action is worthless. They go together. They are inseparable. One without the other is

[5] The definition is proposed by Jaymes P. Morgan in his article 'Why Christian Social Concern?', *Fuller Seminary Theology News and Notes*, December 1967.
[6] Matthew 7:20; John 14:15.

evidence of a deficient Christian life. So we must not try to justify service for our neighbour by claiming that it will 'help us' in our evangelism. God is equally interested in our service and in our evangelistic task. Let us not have a guilty conscience over our schools, hospitals, health centres, student centres, and so on. If they are also used for evangelism, splendid! But let us not use them as a medium of coercion to force the gospel on others. It is not necessary. In themselves they are the expression of Christian maturity.

Political action and evangelism, social action and evangelism, service to the community and evangelism: these are signs of maturity and evidences of a new life. They are a symbol of death to the old life and an evidence of the new. Every cost in terms of sweat and blood, sacrifice, humiliation or persecution for the cause of right and justice will demonstrate that we are crucified with Christ, and not just experts on the doctrine of crucifixion.

The resurrection and the Christian hope

The question is often asked, what is the point of struggling to make a better world if we know that this world is condemned to destruction? With the New Testament we affirm unequivocally that we await a new heaven and a new earth and that the kingdom of God is not a Utopia that man builds up by his own efforts. Christ will establish it when He comes in triumph. But that kingdom is not only in the future. The victory of Christ has already been won in the resurrection and the cross, His triumph over death. The final and total manifestation of the lordship of Christ and the kingdom of God is that for which we long and wait: 'Thy kingdom come.' But we who profess this hope are also witnesses of the operation of His power in our lives here and now. We have been raised in Christ, and we long to do His will each day, just as we wait for that day when it will be done in all the earth, in the whole redeemed creation.[7]

This eschatological hope fills the pages of the New

[7] 1 Corinthians 15; Ephesians 1:15–2:10; Colossians 3; 1 Peter 1:3–5.

Testament. So too the exhortations to a social conduct which is different from and above that of our neighbour are found again and again in the New Testament. We can understand the dynamic of the Christian hope only when we relate these two elements. Obedience to the ethical commands, both individual and social, in the New Testament automatically makes us become the salt and light that makes this world less evil. We have already seen that this obedience is imperative, not optional. Christ is Lord, we cannot have Him as Saviour only. But with all this, we do not believe that the evangelization of the world or our Christian testimony are going to establish the kingdom of God on this earth. That Christ alone will establish in His own time. The guarantee of this final triumph is the victory of the resurrection in which we believe, for, if it were not so, we would be of all men most miserable. The consequences of this in terms of social responsibility are decisive.

The dynamic of a new life

It is the power of God manifested in the resurrection that gives us the new life which we have described as a life of service and obedience to Christ. It is the work of God, not human effort.[8] The tremendous demands of discipleship only God can bring to fruition in us through His Spirit. It is this power of God that lifts us above every sociological situation. It is the power of God that makes us go the second mile. Only in our continual dependence upon Him can we live *in* the world without being *of* the world.

It is lack of faith that leads to monasticism and an anti-biblical separation from the world. It is the fear that contact with the world might stain our lives. The result has been a spirituality which has no contact with this world and which is only possible in the protected shelter of a religious (or evangelical) ghetto. If the spiritual life cannot stand the impact of the temptations to which the politician is subjected, where is the power of the resurrection? It is easy to dogmatize about the wickedness of politicians when we have not even tried to live an upright life in their midst.

[8] Romans 8:11.

It is easy for Christians to be inconsistent at this point. There have been times in which they have felt very keenly the imminence of the return of Christ. Often these are times of social and political crisis or of spiritual coldness and apostasy in the church. The sincerity of this feeling of the imminence of the second coming can be seen in their relation to material things. They have got rid of their possessions at times in a very dramatic fashion.[9] We should emphasize their sincerity because it is in such clear contrast to the attitude of those who use the idea of the return of the Lord as an excuse for not fulfilling the demands of the gospel. For instance, well-to-do people put up massive church buildings so that they will last for centuries, and carry on their businesses with meticulous care, and then talk about the Christian hope to the poor, to the politician who fights for social change, or to the student caught up in the social struggle. This is not only inconsistent, it is converting the gospel into the 'opium of the people'. It is like giving an evangelistic tract to a person who is hungry and then protesting because he eats the tract.

We find the biblical corrective to this attitude in the clear teaching of the apostle Paul. To believe in the return of the Lord and its imminence does not lead one to live in a disorderly way, but to fulfil the requirements of the gospel: 'Let all men know your forbearance. The Lord is at hand.'[1]

The presence and the hope of the kingdom

The citizens of heaven live in earthly kingdoms, with their social structures which may be thoroughly evil. Nevertheless, we proclaim that Christ is Lord: even though at the present time only a few recognize Him as such, His lordship is a fact which soon everyone will see. This same Lord

[9] For example, a book on the origins of the Brethren movement shows how some of its founders, in order to act according to their doctrine concerning prophecy and the world, got rid of their fortunes. This was practised both by individuals and by entire congregations. See Harold H. Rowdon, *The Origins of the Brethren* (Pickering and Inglis, London, 1967), pp. 302–306.
[1] Philippians 4:5; *cf.* 2 Thessalonians 3:6–15.

teaches us to respect the civil authorities of the kingdoms in which we live and to show, in our conduct toward them, who is our true Lord. We accept the State and the social structure as part of God's provision so that man can live upon the earth while the 'time of God's patience' lasts. But our acceptance is not unconditional. If Caesar asks for what belongs to God, we will not give it to him. We know too that it is God supremely who disposes, who puts kings and rulers on the throne, and that all present structure is merely provisional.

The true kingdom will come with Christ at the end, but it is already present here as well, with the presence of those who are His. The provisional State punishes those who do evil. The citizen of the kingdom of God does not return evil for evil. This, for example, together with all the ethical, personal and social duties taught in the New Testament, is a sign that there is a different kingdom which is to come. Those who await that kingdom show it by their conduct. The Christian does not expect to establish the kingdom of God; he waits for the final manifestation of that kingdom which already is a reality. It is for this reason that his conduct is so different, so 'revolutionary'.

> 'Thus he (the Christian) must plunge into social and political problems in order to have an influence on the world, not in the hope of making it a paradise, but simply in order to make it tolerable – not in order to diminish the opposition between this world and the Kingdom of God, but simply in order to modify the opposition between the disorder of this world and the order of preservation that God wills for it – not in order to "bring in" the Kingdom of God, but in order that the Gospel may be proclaimed, that all men may *really* hear the good news of salvation, through the Death and Resurrection of Christ.'[2]

Openness to the future

The hope of the church is not in any temporal kingdom or order of things, nor even in those which Christians may try to establish or to improve. This is why the church does

[2] Jacques Ellul, *The Presence of the Kingdom* (Westminster Press, Philadelphia, 1951), p. 47.

not link its destiny to that of a political, social or economic system. There is no social system that can be called 'Christian' or be considered the expression of Christianity. Each system is better or worse depending on the circumstances, and functions accordingly in keeping with the history and structure of its own country. We do not believe, as some Catholics do, that the return of the communal system of the Middle Ages would be ideal for Latin America. Nor do we believe that *the* evangelical pattern for organizing society is capitalism and the so-called representative democracy.

Latin America is going through a time of crisis and re-evaluation of liberal democratic ideals. We are feeling the weight of the abuse of rich countries in the international marketing of our products. We see how our meagre resources are spent in an arms race that simply follows the changing fortunes of the international cold war. All the power of military governments cannot stop the popular pressure which has been capitalized on by organized terrorism. To what aspect of the *status quo* or of the past can a Christian who reflects upon politics and wants to make his contribution adhere? Be a conservative – of what? Be a revolutionary – for what?

It is in fact the evangelical Christians in Latin America who are better qualified than anyone else to judge the present political situation objectively, if they take seriously the implications of their faith. Without adhering idolatrously to political conservatism or to any particular revolution, the Christian can help determine more clearly what needs to be changed and what must be conserved. For Latin America has to find its own way with realism and dignity.

Again, evangelical presence in areas of practical service can serve as a corrective to the verbosity and demagogism of so much of our politics. Evangelicals ought to explore the possibilities of their presence in projects such as community co-operation, student mobilization for rural or international service, voluntary help in emergency areas, the organization of co-operatives and similar projects.

What better possibility for evangelism than sharing the life of a community in service?

Because his service is obedience to God, because in his life of service he has the help of the Holy Spirit, and because he joyfully awaits the kingdom of God in its final manifestation without fear of the future and within these provisional structures, the Christian can collaborate enthusiastically in the job of bettering his country, and there, in the midst of men, proclaim the Lord who has saved him. There are so many millions today who have not yet known either the love or the transforming power of Christ. Are we really going to match up to our obligations, in evangelism and service?

If we are to do so, it must be by the way of Christ. It is not necessary to abandon the idea of evangelism to fulfil the church's social responsibility. Nor is it necessary to adopt a liberal theology or other ideas that are less than truly biblical and Christian. But service and evangelism must be within actual human situations and social structures. We must 'incarnate' our faith in a given reality, relating our message and the application of that message to it. And our service must be by the way of the cross.

Orientation of the whole of our lives as a vocation of service is the outcome of faith and the new life in Christ. Obedience to Christ in this, too, must lead us to explore the multiple opportunities for service in every society. So often the most urgently-needed social changes will not come just from changed individuals but also from changed social structures.

But we should not expect to build the kingdom of God here on earth or 'Christianize' society. Our hope is future; but at the same time our service and our witness are signs of this hope and of the lordship of Christ in our lives. Certainly Christians are to respect the State and the structures in which they live; but they are not afraid of change, nor do they link the destiny of the church to particular forms of social and political organization. So they are in a better position than any to make a decisive contribution in the midst of the present revolutionary opportunities throughout the world.

Conclusion: the Christian Way
Brian Griffiths

The basic thesis of these essays is that the Christian approach to the problems of modern society is totally different from that of contemporary revolutionary culture. It is not just a slightly different emphasis. It is different at all points – different in its analysis of the cause of the problems, different in its conclusions as to the way in which they should be treated, and different in its estimate of the potential of political and economic change based on revolution.

The one thing both Christians and revolutionaries have in common, however, is an awareness that serious problems exist and that something needs to be done about them. Problems such as poverty, corruption, racism, war, the loss of self, the absence of community, the futility of work and the illusory benefits of technology cry out for solution. But a comparison between the two approaches ends at this point. For the Christian the claim that these problems are the product of certain types of society is true only in a very limited and superficial sense. They can properly be understood, he feels, only as part of a world which was created by God for our good, but which has been fundamentally disrupted as a result of the Fall.

The Bible is quite explicit in teaching that man was created in the image of God and that the material universe was intended for his use and enjoyment. The divine mandate was for man to control his environment, to live in community with his fellow human beings, to recognize his position in relation to his Creator and, because of that recognition, to experience a unique relationship with God. This was not something 'outside' or 'above' his physical environment. Rather, his worship of his Creator, which was his *raison d'être*, was to take place through all his activities. This is very important, for the Christian can never argue either that the material world is essentially evil and to be withdrawn from, which is the approach of monasticism, or that aesthetic activity, contemplation and the 'higher' things of life are superior to the physical.

But equally crucial to understanding our society is the Fall and its cataclysmic effect on society. The harmony which previously existed between God, man, the physical universe and society was totally disrupted because of sin. To the Christian, therefore, man's alienation from man is ultimately a result of man's alienation from God. The importance of sin in our understanding, not only of ourselves but also of our society, cannot be emphasized enough. If this, then, is the root of the problem, and not simply capitalism, or bureaucracy or urbanization, it is hardly surprising that the advocacy of revolution as a panacea is something which must be categorically rejected.

While revolution may create new social institutions and destroy old ones, it is powerless to change human nature. Revolution *is* change, but only in a very restricted sense. Undoubtedly the weakest aspect of contemporary revolutionary doctrine is the notion that the way to create new dimensions to human life is by changing social institutions, whether it be through the attempt to abolish class, to effect workers' control of industry, to destroy the State, to get rid of bureaucracy or to reject affluence and urbanization in favour of a community closer to nature. 'Integral human freedom will at last be possible.' But will it? What scrap of historical evidence is there to suggest that the basic quality of life will be radically changed by changing social institutions in this way? Has it been achieved through the revolutions of Russia, Cuba or China? Was it achieved in France after 1789? Is there any evidence from anthropology to show that the quality of life is fundamentally different in primitive tribes? Was the experiment in the setting up of the Paris Commune in 1871 the outstanding success its supporters claimed it would be? In more recent times what about Haight-Asbury? An extremely useful Christian contribution would be to document these experiments in detail showing the intellectual and moral bases on which they were constructed, the incredible optimism of their supporters, their positive successes, the reasons for the ultimate failure and finally the human suffering and tragedy which resulted. From what we already know of these experiments, such a study would surely show humanity's constant optimism of what can be achieved by revolution and so lend support to Hegel's dictum that 'History teaches us that history teaches us nothing'. Contemporary exponents of revolution simply cannot approach history with an honest and open mind and then argue that their thesis is built on it and not in spite of it.

If revolution is so categorically rejected, what then is the Christian way? As these essays have pointed out, the Christian starts not with society and its problems but with the individual. It is he himself who first needs to be changed – and not just superficially, but radically. Changed so that he is no longer the slave of his consuming ambitions; changed so that he can live at peace with himself; changed so that he is honest, unselfish, with a genuine concern for others; changed so that life has a purpose and work is part of his worship. Change for the Christian is the liberation of man from a dominant sinful nature so that he has the possibility of choosing good. And this can come only by the recognition of his own sin before God, a real and deep repentance of his condition and acceptance of what Jesus Christ has done on his behalf.

Jesus Christ said 'If you continue in my word, you are truly my disciples, and you will know the truth, and the truth will make you free'.[1] In a related passage He states

[1] John 8:31, 32, RSV.

quite unequivocally that for a man to be free he must experience a new birth. Nothing could be more radical than this analogy. On both occasions, however, He was met by total incomprehension. The intelligent Jewish lawyer and politician, Nicodemus, retorted, 'But how is it possible for a man to be born when he is old? Can he enter his mother's womb a second time and be born?'[2] His answer substantiates its importance, however, and shows it to be at the very centre of His teaching.

This concern with the individual and the importance of personal commitment might be taken to mean that the Christian is unconcerned with the problem of society as a whole, its particular structures and the ways in which they may be changed. Nothing could be further from the truth, however. Without exception the basic argument of each of these essays is that the Christian has a clear mandate to be involved in the total life of society; social, political, economic and cultural. The activities of a Christian cannot be neatly dichotomized into the world and the church, with the implicit prescription that he must withdraw from the evils of the one to the seclusion of the other. The challenge of an individual Christian is to play his part in all aspects of the life of society, always seeking in whatever he does to be honest before God and sincerely to care for and love his neighbour as himself. Depending on interest and ability he (she) will be involved in all facets of the life of society, whether it be as a suburban housewife organizing a playgroup, a conservationist campaigning for the protection of the environment, a trade unionist representing his fellow workers, a student giving time to the Students Union and student societies, or an elected representative on a local council or in parliament.

In his specific concern with political issues such as industrial relations, fiscal policy, foreign affairs, education, welfare and so forth, the contribution of the Christian is not as a political revolutionary. This would be in outright contradiction of the life of our Lord as well as of the whole of biblical teaching. Based on the principle that we are to

[2] John 3:4, NEB.

render to Caesar what is Caesar's, the distinctive contribution of the Christian will be that of a reformer, a proponent of gradual change, who seeks to alter and modify the system from within. But even his aims and aspirations for social policy cannot be independent of God's revelation. Whatever political causes he embraces and whatever changes he suggests must ultimately be compatible with such biblical principles as individualism, justice, honesty, equality of all in the sight of God, a concern for the poor and under-privileged and a respect for property and authority. While these principles do not imply a unique political programme resulting in a specifically Christian political party, they most definitely limit the range of political alternatives which are available and suggest that the spirit in which some change is called for may be as important as the change itself.

On the other hand, though the individual Christian has a clear duty to be involved, the church *qua* church, should not be involved if that involvement necessitates its taking up a political position. The prime duty of the church is to pro-claim those eternal truths which hold true regardless of the characteristics of the society. The church certainly has a res-ponsibility in its teaching to present the Christian ethic for society. It should speak out against all forms of evil, racism, torture, propaganda, the abuse of power, in fact anything which is clearly contrary to our Lord's teaching. But if as an institution it aligned itself to a specific *political* programme to combat any of these, it is almost certain it would jeopardize its proclamation of the only true gospel, which ultimately is its *raison d'être*.

In conclusion we come back to the question, Is revolution change? The Christian is profoundly sceptical that a revolution which causes a major political or economic upheaval will change society for the better. Certainly both history and the Bible offer little supportive evidence. For the Christian the ray of hope shines through at the individual level. Individuals' lives can be revolutionized. And through the unglamorous daily round of individuals living out their Christian lives, ultimately society itself can be renewed and changed.

> 'You are light for all the world.... And you ... must shed light among your fellows, so that, when they see the good you do, they may give praise to your Father in heaven.'[3]

[3] Matthew 5:14–16, NEB.